SHIELD-MAIDEN PUBLISHING AUSTRALIA PTY LTD

www.shieldmaidenpublishing.com

Special thanks to Sally-Anne Ward at Three Little Birds Press

"Even if a fool lived with a wise man all his life,
he would still not recognize the truth, like a wooden
spoon cannot recognize the flavor of the soup"

Buddhist Scriptures

Special Thanks

To my beautiful Nick,
You have made life worth living
And I cherish every precious moment
I can gaze into your eyes and feel Loved.
To Freya, Nova & Archie
For accepting you have a crazy Mama,
For loving me anyway, and for
Making life worth living.
To my dogs,
Better than most humans and
Always by my side, thank you
For the constant companionship & Love.
Woof

I was born on December 22nd 1969 in Bromsgrove,
Worcestershire, England to my parents Daniel and Margaret. I
weighed 7lbs 7oz and came into the World with a mass of
dark hair and a cheeky smile. On Christmas Eve when the
hospital released my Mother to go home for Christmas, she
left without me, exclaiming half a mile down the road to my
controlling German Grandfather,

OMG! The baby!

Luckily, he turned the car around. My Mother was only
twenty years old when I was born, barely a woman herself,
and in some ways, it felt like we grew up together. But I was
born an old soul, always feeling older than everyone around
me even when I was five years old. My strange demeanor
often worked against me, as it betrayed a deep knowing that
some adults found both confusing and magnetic. I was quiet,
sullen and always serious. I remember many people telling me
to *Cheer up will you!* as a child, never realizing that though I
was present in the room with them, I was in fact trapped.

Trapped behind my next-door neighbor's couch, and I would remain there for many years.

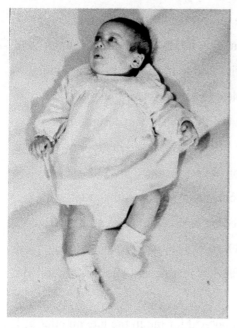

(PHOTO: My Son Archie says I was born pouting.)

Everyone I have ever known has some kind of addiction, drugs, alcohol, smoking, sex, rage, social media, food, virtue signaling, bullying, stalking, shopping, gambling or multiple combinations of such. My addiction has always been working.

I think it happened because there was so much arguing at home between my parents that I literally ran out of the door to school because school was my haven of peace. Can you imagine that, a massive, noisy, brat-filled school was my sanctuary? Even on Sunday's I didn't want to be at home, and so even though the stories told to me about Jesus at Sunday School felt like Fairytales, I never missed it just for the opportunity of being out of the house. The definition of a workaholic is someone who always has to be doing something and that became me from a very young age. As I grew my life became a series of quite bi-polar points on the graph with some of the memories being reasonably unpleasant and some fantastically brilliant. There is a saying that the entertainment industry brings either feast or famine and I am here to tell you that is absolutely true.

A light bulb moment happened for me in the late nineties as I sat in the greenroom of a TV show I was filming. An actress who had been keeping her weight down by snorting speed had passed out on one of the couches and I was sitting holding her frail and boney hand as I listened to the ambulance getting ever closer. Her cheekbones jutted out of her face at prominent angles and her teeth looked too big for her tiny childlike head. She was approximately 23 years old and I could already see what she would look like as an old woman, ravaged as she was by drug use and anorexia. I had worked my arse off to get in that room and be in that position, but as I sat there holding her limp hand, I told myself something surprising, I told myself, "Nic, you're better than this."

I had reached the top, a prominent role on a massively popular TV soap opera, but after reaching a goal I had never thought possible I suddenly realized that it wasn't making me happy, and that it never would. When I speak it out loud, I always say that I am a *Glass half-full* girl, except inside I am not. Inside I am always waiting for someone to fuck me over, and sure enough 99 times out of 100 they usually do. I guess you could say that my negativity brings that outcome upon me, but I choose not to believe that. Instead, I have spent my life searching for what was missing in my childhood - happiness, authenticity and security. Like most of you out there I needed human connection and love, because my love battery was decidedly empty, in fact I'm not entirely sure it had ever been fully charged. *Fame* can sometimes feel like love, all the right things are said to you and people fight to be in your presence as they bask in the reflected glory that shines upon them. They claim you are *family* and they will always be there for you no matter what, but after the fame and the money are all gone, or no longer sought or expected by you, their *love* mysteriously evaporates. It's a crap feeling, like being the most popular girl in school and then shitting your pants in Math's class and suddenly nobody wants anything to do with you anymore, it's that brutal. You are yesterday's news, a *has-been* and no matter how much you recite the fame mantra of *it's better to be a has-been than a never-was* it still hurts. If that wasn't bad enough there is aging in front of camera. In real life I am well aware when I'm having a bad hair or skin day and I make sure to avoid mirrors, but there is no hiding place under a grid of television lighting and three different angles of your face on the World's most expensive studio cameras. Even a stray hair that may be jutting out of your face gets its fifteen minutes of fame. I once saw a spit-bridge appear in the playback of a shot following an onscreen kiss. I wanted the floor to open up and swallow me when I heard the Director yell,

Yep! That's the one!

Joan Collins said it best.

Being born beautiful is like being born rich and gradually growing poorer.

I had hoped fame would become the warm cushion of love around me that had been sadly lacking, but when it arrived it did nothing of the sort. Instead, it felt intrusive, critical and demanding. There literally wasn't enough of me to go around and groups of fans would beg for photos and autographs at the studio gates making me feel like an absolute jerk when after fourteen hours of filming I'd simply burn past them in a hurry to get home, flooring my range rover to the sound of their screams *"OMG SARAH!"* as their excitement slowly dimmed in the distance behind me. I always wished there could be a spare Nicola Charles to do the things the fans demanded of me, while the real me continued filming.

I began developing Agoraphobia.

The term describes the fear of places or situations that might cause panic, helplessness or embarrassment, and is an anxiety

6

disorder. From my best recollection mine began in 1998 when during a personal appearance at the 21st Century nightclub in Frankston, Melbourne, a girl became wedged in a hoard of screaming fans who were being rotated on a revolving dance floor and after becoming trapped she fell and broke her arm. Her piercing scream of agony in one moment changed me. I yelled over the PA system like a drill sergeant for the crowds to calm down and stop pushing. The room became silent as suddenly the crowd were woken from their delusions and snapped into the reality that the person standing there on the stage was in fact Nicola Charles and *not* Sarah Beaumont. I know I said something surprising to them that night, something they hadn't expected to hear, and the brutality of it would become almost a trademark for every public address I would make in my lifetime, because I told the truth.
I yelled,

Please stop pushing this is ridiculous! A girl has been hurt! I am a normal human being just like you! Calm down right now or I'm leaving!

It definitely brought us all back down to earth pretty fast, and as a Capricorn that's exactly where I wanted my life to be, grounded as solidly to the earth as possible. Minutes later my request for calm was all but forgotten and mayhem again ensued, and I remember becoming distraught and being carried out of there by a large security guard who held me above his head like a tray of sushi. But my Agoraphobia having been brought on by rushing crowds and compounded with global fame became an issue in many other areas of my life too. I became a hermit, with my therapist saying I was also a *Misanthrope*, someone who avoids human society. Suddenly even going to the supermarket felt intrusive, someone would see me, and know me, and follow me around. They would analyze what was in my trolley, ask me about storylines and yell across aisles that they had spotted Sarah Beaumont *shopping!* More often than not I would go without my longed-for Turkey slices as a snack, because getting them felt like too much like a chore. I said no to nine out of ten social engagements, whether they be publicity, work related or personal, and photo shoots became a new hell that hit me like a steam train. As a model I had been cast to be *exactly* what the client had asked for, usually a *girl-next-door* type to sell

Oil of Olay or *Ford Cars* etc. But as a *Celebrity* the standard was vastly different. Stylists and photographers would make comments like,

We need to make you look as thin as possible! You're very curvaceous!

The comments were made to ignite guilt in me about my size, and it worked, as I struggled to find angles that would see me fall in line with what I was being told magazines *needed*. I was suddenly sub-standard for TV having missed the anorexia bar by about fourteen pounds. *Body Dysmorphic Disorder* began to touch my life and despite being told I was *very light* for my height by my doctor was clearly not slim enough for TV. Every glance from every human became a critical dagger, every sigh from a cameraman a cause for anxiety, and every outfit that wardrobe squeezed me into was like overcoming a date with Satan, terrifying.

I was 25 and had the body of a 25-year-old, and yet it was becoming increasingly apparent that what was required was a 25-year-old with the body of a 16-year-old, and I knew the clock was ticking because my curves were going nowhere fast.

I remember once asking the wardrobe mistress why my outfits resembled napkins and was told,

What do you think they are paying you for? It's your pound of flesh.

The double standards in acting were blinding and her face betrayed a splinter of sympathy. No-one ever considered the size and shape of Philip Seymour Hoffman, not even during naked sex scenes with phenomenally beautiful female actresses, because women have for too long been held to a ridiculous standard that harks back to the strange ideals of that bastion of morality, Hollywood. For actresses there are only two categories, and whether you play the hottie at the office or the young Mum of two kids, you must always fall into either the *impossibly thin and gorgeous* mold OR *a big girl who is lots of fun so how could you not love and adore her?* Strangely an extra hundred pounds was fine, but an extra fourteen…? absolutely not. So, what was required for the profession seemed to be *a lot* of weight loss, leading to the inevitable boob job, because we all know what disappears first when we lose weight.

And so there I was, a literal square peg in a round hole because I fitted neither category, I was simply what I had always been *a girl-next-door type*, not fat, not thin, just normal, and there was no way I was having breast implants. Whilst loving the craft of acting and bringing a character to life I was finding *Fame* very much like one of my characters outfits, an ill fit, and so questions dominated my professional considerations, questions like, where would I go from here? Where does anyone go when they have reached their desired goal only to learn it wasn't quite what they'd expected? So like many introverted actors before me I began to try the escapism of drugs and alcohol, and that journey would culminate in a very scary point on the graph that circled me back to the greenroom and that frail, boney hand.

And so what of the journey through life that got me *there?* What of the cast of adults in my real life that had contributed to it all? They were nothing short of a wretched hive of villains, tyrants and perverts. This was my England, my home, my beginnings, and my earliest memories of it haunt me still to this day.

I have always loved dogs, but what I loved more than dogs as a child was horses, and when I was eight years old my Mother bought me a Palomino pony I named *Goldie.* She was a scrawny little thing and wasn't going to grow much taller than thirteen hands in height, but to me she was perfect. Unlike many Palomino's she had no walleyes and instead had large brown eyes framed by extremely long lashes. She was my living, breathing Barbie horse and I loved her dearly.

(PHOTO: Mum, Me aged seven & Goldie as a foal on the Farm. I think Mum knew I needed a friend that wasn't a human.)

I remember telling her about my wicked next-door Neighbour and how he had thrown me to the ground behind his couch one

Saturday afternoon and pushed his finger between my legs and inside me. I told her about the physical pain and the unfamiliar smell that was on his hands when he removed them from me, and that I didn't understand any of it. I would treat my chats with *Goldie* as therapy, and unsurprisingly she was an extremely patient listener. I was five years old when the assault had occurred and as per the instructions of my paedophile neighbour I never told a soul.

(PHOTO: This was one of my last memories before the assault. It's one of the last photos you will find of me smiling

too. Whatever magic life had placed inside me, the magic and
innocence all children have, was stolen from me, and never
came back.)

(PHOTO: I had done no harm to anyone. How could I have?
I was a small child. And yet the Universe had a different plan
for me, one that I am not alone in suffering through.)
I really had no choice because this stella member of my
community had told me that he would *kill my Dad* if I told

anyone. I used to watch my Dad tinkering with his motorbikes, making fiberglass body parts for his bike in his shed.

(PHOTO: Dad on his bike at either Silverstone or Brands Hatch, England. Can't remember which. I think he spent years trying to beat Barry Sheene. Never did.)

He certainly didn't deserve to die at the hands of a pedophile who had hurt me for a few minutes, that was my five-year-old reasoning anyway. After the assault I used to do a whole heap of dangerous and almost suicidal stuff because I guess a small part of me wanted to die. I know I felt broken and useless, and convinced that if anyone in the real World knew of my dirty little secret nobody would want anything to do with me. Even at that tender age, I knew that as the victim I would be blamed, and that any female that speaks out is instantly accused of seeking *Victimhood.* This betrayal of morality is what breathes freedom into the behaviors of Paedophiles and the malevolence of silence became a scar inside me for half a century.

I remember a giant eight-lane freeway was being built straight through our beautiful piece of the English countryside. Monstrously huge Caterpillar earth movers lay dormant overnight and my friend and I would go and measure ourselves against the giant tyres on the vehicles, marveling that we would need to be six times taller to be as tall as just the tyre!

(PHOTO: My Brother and I climbing all over some heavy piece of machinery someone had left in a field near us. Looks like a Tank! I wasn't like other girls. Post sexual assault my demeanor was flat and morose. I tried so hard to yank myself back to where I was before him, but I was never successful.)

Beneath the giant yellow mechanical monsters and below the muddy layout of the freeway lay drainage tunnels. Their walls were covered in shiny, black corrugated plastic that smelled like rubber, and looking from one side to the other only a tiny dot of light was visible. I had an urge to crawl through it. The freeway hadn't even been built yet, and the tunnels could have collapsed at any time, but I guess if they had, I wouldn't be telling you my life story now. As it was, I made it to the other side, with my friend yelling at me constantly to *"GET A MOVE ON!"* My heart raced with a mixture of fear and excitement and it would become a metaphor for the many risks I was prepared to take in life from that point on. Looking back, it's as if the adversity of the assault had changed my brain chemistry. I became a daredevil, a risk taker, a deal maker and someone who lived very close to the edge. Knowing that these behaviors had begun as early as six years old still terrifies me to this day, especially the knowledge that I had put myself in harms way multiple times as a child, and yet despite several near misses, simply kept taking risks. Perhaps I *was* baiting death. Perhaps I had lost value in my own life, or perhaps the value of it had been taken from me.

The worst part for me was learning much later on that perhaps my father and my abuser were brothers in arms. That fact is a like a spinning sphere covered in knives. If I try and open it, I know I'll be badly hurt. Could he have given me to this Monster? It's something I can never know, and I'm not entirely sure I want to.

2

When I was nine years old, I ran away from home. It was my Brothers seventh Birthday and to my shame I simply couldn't cope with all the attention he was getting. He had been such a naughty child and to me seemed to get all of my parent's attention for all the wrong reasons. While I would get good grades at school, he would bunk off and run around with his mates, he'd steal the guns from my Dad's gun cabinet without consequence and my parents would spend hours and hours arguing about it and talking to him, all while I sat silently doing my English and History homework. I began having thoughts that I might like him to meet with a terrible accident so I could be an only child, or perhaps find out that I was adopted and my real family were fabulously wealthy and interesting, and if I just sat tight, they would eventually come back for me. As a toddler I had apparently already let my Brother fall from the couch to the floor as a baby without trying to help, so I get the feeling that I was never really a fan.

(PHOTO: With my Brother when we were very young, dressed immaculately as always. Mum certainly had an eye for kids clothing.)

But as is often the case between Mothers and Sons he became the favorite child and I went back to having endless discussions inside my own head about it. It taught me early on to accept the fact that nice guys do indeed often *finish last,* particularly if that guy is *a girl.* My parent's marriage was a larva-covered mountain of fire and passion, and I have a very strong memory of the most loving moment I ever saw between them. Mum was washing up at the kitchen sink and my Dad walked up behind her, looped his arms under hers and grabbed her boobs. Even though I was a child I remember thinking *I want to be loved like that* as I watched her giggle and push him away with her soapy hands. But my Dad's hideous amounts of infidelity put paid to all that love and passion, and in the end my Mother simply couldn't take it anymore. She would take me on ride alongs to drag him from the arms of other women, ropey looking women at that, and I remember thinking *I love you, but you're a prick.* The *leaving* part of their marriage was extremely distressing but not totally uncommon. He stood at the door on Christmas Eve *threatening* to go with my Mum on her hands and knees begging him to stay for the sake of the children, whilst pulling at the bottom of his trousers. In that moment I told myself *No. I will never do THAT* as it was very much beneath her to beg, and she deserved much better. To this day Christmas is a very difficult and sensitive time of year for me and I struggle constantly. It is very much noticed and noted by anyone around me during that time of year and they often say they are saddened that the pain remains after so many years. Robbed of the happy Christmas memories we are supposed to carry from childhood, remembering only the bad, I attempt to recreate happier memories, usually setting myself up for failure, when life doesn't quite live up to my expectations. Ridiculous and meaningless things can trigger it. One year my husband at the time gave me Toothpaste as a Christmas gift, followed the next year by a kitchen plate drainer. It wouldn't end well for him. I would tell myself no-one was filling the Daddy-love void and no-one was even thoughtful enough to try. It's a messy and confusing time with my own behaviors often feeling embarrassing and at the same time unconscious and uncontrollable.

The Christmas that he left us my Mother got drunk on Whiskey *something I had never seen her drink* and my late Grandmother came over and picked up the pieces.

*(PHOTO: My German Grandfather Siegfried and my
Grandmother Amy-Louise. She loved him endlessly but like
my own father he loved many and they eventually divorced.
She remained alone until her death and stood by my Mother's
side during my parents divorce. I never heard my
Grandmother raise her voice, not once. She was a lady in the
true sense of the word. I miss her so much and spoke to her
from Australia two weeks before her passing. She is definitely
my Guardian Angel. Often when things seem too much and I
just need that small piece of Luck it comes along, and I firmly
believe she's behind it.)*

24

I always knew my Mother would meet someone else and be okay as she is one of the more interesting people I've known in my life, and growing up with her meant there was never a dull moment. Sometimes I would meet other Mum's and think them something of a vegetable compared to my crazy Mum. The older I get the more I appreciate that whatever happened to my Mum she always survived, and it placed a strength in me that has never died.

But the truly crazy side of me, the side that sees things just a little bit differently, is surely the side I inherited from my Dad. As a very practical and pragmatic woman from German descent my Mum used to say that he had *Delusions of Grandeur*. This was because he was adopted under very suspicious and intriguing circumstances and because of that he had become obsessed with who he was and where he came from, tracking down one possibility that he was the illegitimate Son of a Hollywood movie star who was filming at Pinewood Film Studios in London. One of the points of contention in my parent's marriage was his fierce will to discover the truth about this and his birth parents generally. I remember one argument over his spending thousands of pounds on phone bills after months of calling registrars of births, deaths and marriages up and down the country looking for his longed-for answers, long before the internet and the ease of sites like Ancestry dot com existed. It was during that time that I began questioning his sanity because here had been a Dad who was a worker and a player, someone who had ridden his Norton race bike at Silverstone and Brands Hatch every other weekend, not someone who would ever find a fascination in dark forces, and yet he became obsessed with the Occult. In the end his spiral down into the maelstrom was all far more than my Mother could stand. She simply couldn't take the lunacy of it anymore, and I believe her love for him died. Everyone has a limit, and my Mother had reached hers. Women are a bit like that, despite communicating to our partners that certain behaviors are driving us away, we accept that they rarely listen, and that they only realize when it's too late.

I began for the first time feeling concerned when my father and I went shooting. He had been asked to be a kind of Shepherd for an elderly Farmer who lived close to us. The Farmer was losing sheep to foxes and at 96 years old didn't have a super flash aim with his shotgun anymore. I think it's safe to say we were all relieved when Gilbert and his white eyes full of cataracts no longer swung his double barreled 12 bore shotgun around anymore. I have looked down the large barrels of guns so many times in my life and wondered *is it now?* The first time I fired a 12 bore shotgun it almost smashed my collarbone as it kicked back so violently, but the smell of the red and gold spent cartridges that flew out of the chamber was strangely intoxicating. The boom of gunfire was unlike anything else I had ever heard up close. It was the sound of *Finality*. Whatever was in the way was finished, and for all the rhetoric around guns and their uses there is no denying they are a manmade wonder that has fed us, protected us and enabled us to live in a dangerous World of predators that would hunt us without conscience. Holding a gun feels like power, and in the wrong hands is devastating. Was my Dads gun in the wrong hands? I often wondered. Most conversations I had with him during childhood weren't about anything important, they were always about guns and ammo. I had always trusted my Dad implicitly up to that point but as I witnessed his mental health decline, I began to feel instinctively unsafe. Suddenly sitting alone with this man I had been conditioned to trust as he sobbed while wiping down two shotgun barrels with an oily rag gave me pause. There was a crippling inevitability about his life and therefore mine, as I felt strongly that his mental health issues would probably run downhill. There wasn't going to be any happy endings for him, he was too far-gone, and there was nothing I could do to save him. Now, as an adult I would have known exactly the kind of conversation to have with him and that knowledge breaks my heart. Years later when I learned of his death his partner of many years said to me, *Well at least you got to have your reunion at Heathrow Airport before he passed.* He had told her that a couple of years earlier he and I had met at a Heathrow Airport Hotel for a big reunion as I was connecting through to the USA. That my children were with me, and that it was wonderful. Except there had been no reunion, and my blood ran cold as she described his delight at the meeting in remarkable detail. Perhaps he had needed to fabricate such a meeting in his head to cope, perhaps he had wanted it so badly that his mind had made it a reality, or perhaps he had as expected left his marbles long behind in the hell he had been plunged into when discovering he was adopted. I have a mortal fear that my father is waiting for me at the top of that frozen hillside in Worcestershire wearing his green hunting sweater with leather elbow patches, holding his 12 bore shotgun under his arm with the stock sticking out back and the barrels cocked down in front, his hand outstretched to take me to the next place. This recurring image gives me *fear of death*. I had learned of his passing through a direct message on twitter. The British Police had contacted me to say they had important information about a family member. It was an extremely painful and shocking way to find out, and I suddenly realized that all those questions I had for him, all the things I had bottled up for years, rolled up in the anger and resentment I had felt, were never going to be answered. I knew I had screwed up. It wouldn't have taken much to find him and discuss it, and I'll have to live with that regret for the rest of my life.

(PHOTO: The three of us, Steve, Dad and I at the beach. I loved and adored him and never imagined I'd have to exist without him.)

After he had left us, it was tough being at school and hearing the conversations between other girls, conversations that involved phrases like *My Dad is taking me to blah blah blah* or *My Dad bought me this for Christmas.* I had no Dad and even when he had been physically in our lives, he was too distant to reach. I told myself it was something I had done that had caused all this, that I wasn't a good enough Daughter, or that our family hadn't made him happy enough. It's been 39

30

years since my Dad walked out the door, and I still have unanswered questions, so I tell anyone who will listen and still has their parents with them to make the most of the time, for they are very lucky. I felt it was the easy and selfish way out to crack up and make it all about him. I didn't mind that he left, at least the arguing stopped, but to never be in my life again was like a dagger and I would recommend that all *Leavers* make sure they explain their decision comprehensively to their kids when they are old enough to understand, so they are not left languishing with confusing memories about *what happened* as adults. Most of us know that after children, no matter how tough things get, we hold it together for our kids. I should have let all that anger go, forgiven him, and asked about the truth, but like so many others who make the same mistake it's all too late now. And so it was time for me to get tough and go it alone. Fatherless and in an unusually tense relationship with my own Mother I wanted to know what the World was really like, outside the walls of my own family, and I became determined to find out.

Despite being academically minded the school projects that got the most attention were in Art. Large pencil drawings of grim scenes that included much death and destruction lay around my bedroom, but they also hung on school walls, as first my teacher and then my Head Teacher took a shine to them. I was hauled in and told that I needed to go on to do a degree in Art and that I *Owed it to the World* to share my talent. For a while I accepted this line of thinking and looked into courses on Theatre Set Design, Art History and Fine Art. However, the prospectus also had a Business & Finance Degree on offer and I was reasonably sure my exam results would give me the criteria to qualify for it. After all this was the late eighties and I had been something of a rebel and taken *Computer Studies*. In a last gasp I put down the 2B Pencils and jumped from Art to Business, literally on *instinct*. I will never forget the comment my Mother made when I told her I had signed up for Business & Finance instead of Fine Art.

Why would you do a thing like that? You're a pretty enough girl you should just find a man who is wealthy.

She can never have known the lifelong impact that dismissive comment left on me. In a passionate and childish rebellion against my Mother I would thwart the advances of wealthy men for the rest of my life just to rebel against her.

(PHOTO: Mum and I in the garden. She was a loud and confident German Mum. I was happy to play the side-kick.)

The course was hideously tedious.

Far from exciting my mind about the World of Business it felt like an indoctrination into drudgery as I slowly became ground down by the endless Economics classes and broke the tedium by applying for the jobs, I had hoped my business degree would help me achieve, only I was applying for them before having my actual degree, and to my complete surprise job interviews were offered, and so during the final year of my degree course I dropped out of college to *go to work*. Though the decision seems in hindsight reckless and self-destructive it actually became the making of me. I was constantly chasing my tail knowing that I had to work harder and smarter than those who would be coming up behind me degrees in hand, but I would now have that thing that is prized far more than pieces of paper with degrees on them, I had *work experience*. My first role took me into banking, mortgages to be exact. It required a 1hr train ride alone in the dark every morning from Worcestershire into the British city of Birmingham, and the Head Office of a major British Bank. Suddenly I was part of the adult World and quickly worked out that making money was actually a lot easier than I had anticipated. Because I had joined the team during the UK's Mortgage Boom in the early

90's my role allowed me the option of working *flexitime* and so I began working from 7am to 7pm five days a week. It was one of the best feelings in the World to be able to walk up to any ATM in any town or city and have access to my own money, and making money quickly became *my addiction* at the tender age of 19.

Happy with my access to cash I hadn't really considered moving careers or jobs, and working for a major UK Bank meant that I could potentially have a job for life. Many of my former colleagues at the Bank recently retired and had spent their entire lives in one role. I would often be pulled aside by senior managers and told that with my work ethic, personality and social skills I would likely be running my own regional branch of the Bank by the time I was 30. It's funny, but the mental picture of that suddenly didn't seem so great, and like most of us when we picture a future for ourselves, I began to wonder if that achievement in life would ever be enough. An unknown cog in a large financial machine, sitting behind a desk, a computer screen and the same four walls for life felt remarkably uninspiring for a girl who had been through so much, in fact the notion of it felt a bit like a prison sentence.

All the same I soldiered on and became well known for being a worker-bee who clocked in more hours than most, first in and last home as I watched the numbers in my bank account slowly go up.

As well as my pony another childhood hobby had been dancing. I attended classes religiously every weekend and even became a member of the Dance Academy's troop, always standing in the back-row as I was one of the tallest, I remember dancing in competitions so hard and so fast that I thought my heart might stop. Our troop was called *Scaramoosh* and every dancer at the school wanted to be in the troop. The memories are a blur of flying sequins and leg kicks followed by bottle after bottle of Coca-Cola drunk through that non-PC killer of planets, plastic straws. So when a friend from the troop asked me to accompany her to London on a daytrip because she was auditioning at Pineapple Dance Studio in Covent Garden for a musical role the nostalgia of it saw me agree to go.

I had always been a country girl, and still to this day the countryside is where I long to be. I don't like the concrete jungle and instead long for trees, green fields and a chance to see the seasons changing, but somehow Covent Garden felt surprisingly like a good fit. The cobbled streets, the ritzy shops and café bars opened up a World to me I didn't know existed, and I got a strange feeling of Déjà vu, as if I had been there before. It was Christmas time and the streets were filled with twinkling lights swinging in the chilly breeze. Shop windows were filled with animatronic Santa's and The Grinch and in truth the feeling of it being a second home was starting to freak me out. Fate was drawing me to this place, even though the trip had been nothing to do with me. The line for the audition was long and stretched all the way around the building. Despite being winter it was a warmish day for the UK and so we all sat on our bags on the cobbles chatting as slowly the line moved into the alleyway outside Pineapple Dance Studio. As my friend began stretching and warming up for her audition I walked up and down the side street to stretch my legs and to see what lay at either end. Then, as I turned back to join her in the line a tall well dressed blonde gentlemen was walking towards me smiling as if he knew me. It was most disconcerting as a 19-year-old in a big city and so nervously I kept walking and smiled back. I couldn't have known it was the most important smile of my lifetime and as I did his face ran over with an expression of delight and he began making his way towards me. I was in no danger, the street was full of dancers leaning on walls and jumping up and down to warm up for their auditions, and so I was intrigued by what he was going to say. Maybe he too was a stranger in this city and was looking for directions? But what came out of his mouth changed the course of my life forever, and he became another point on the graph of who I became and how I got here.

He said, in a rather lovely Scottish accent:

Hello! I am the Chief Executive of Coca-Cola UK and I was wondering if you would do me the honor of attending an audition tomorrow? We are casting for the lead role in a major new TV campaign?

Perplexed, immature and nervous by the request I told him I wouldn't be in London tomorrow as it was just a day trip.

He began scribbling an address on the back of his business card and as he handed it to me, he said,

I strongly suggest you grab a room for the night and come here tomorrow at 10. I think you'll be very pleased with the outcome.

And so I did.

I mean how often do girls get stopped in the street in London and asked to audition for a major TV commercial? I'd have been insane not to do it.

Having overheard the entire exchange the fame-hungry dancers still stretching and queuing in line outside Pineapple dance studio looked me up and down begrudgingly, questioning what it was about me that had caught this man's attention, and for the life of me I certainly didn't know.

I only had one job during the audition. Nothing like my job at the bank which involved dragging my tired arse out of bed at 5am in the darkness to catch the 6am train from Worcestershire to Birmingham, nothing like trawling through acres of microfiche looking for customer details and records on their mortgage payments and nothing like sharing a bathroom with over 600 employees for 12 hours a day. No nothing like that at all, in fact I was made to feel very special indeed.

The casting suite was small and in one of those cute London Mews Houses that had been converted for the purpose. I confidently walked through the massive navy-blue door and up the small, threadbare carpeted stairway. The stairs creaked like something from an old horror movie with every step I took, betraying the age of this adorable mews house, and the sound somehow added to the tension of the unusual situation I was now facing. The receptionist made me feel like a movie star and had clearly been prepped that someone was attending who had been invited by the Chief Executive, and the whole thing was just about the most pleasant work experience I'd ever had. It was easy, almost too easy.

I sat in front of the bright blue screen in a tiny room and looked into the lens of the film camera. I could see the focus changing inside the glass circle as it zoomed in close on my 19-year-old face. The room was warm and comfortable and the same man who had stopped me in the street directed me on what to do as three other men sat silently along the wall behind him, only lifting their hands for a brief wave as I entered.

He said in that beautiful Scottish accent:
Nicola, it's very simple, all I want you to do is pick up that can of Sprite in front of you, take a drink from it and then placing it back on the table in front, smile at camera.

I did it.
Just once.
And that was all it took.
He joyfully clapped his hands together and said to the other people in the room,

I knew it!
Ladies and Gentlemen, we now have our Sprite Kids!

Smiling into that camera was about to earn me over 100,000 UK pounds, and so once home, and with Bronski Beat's Smalltown Boy on a never-ending loop in my head, I ran away to London to become a model. Because discovering that *one* commercial that was estimated to take ten days to film, would earn me three times my annual salary at the bank was a total game-changer.

The commercial was supposed to be a ten-day shoot in Lake Garda, Italy, but it became blatantly obvious when we got there that the torrential rain had other ideas. All the same the scenery on the Lake was breathtaking. Tiny dots of people could be seen skiing high above on the mountains surrounding the lake, while boats and tourists motored up and down the vast waters that rippled like an ocean in front of the very grand Five Star Hotel we were staying at. The foyer had a large black grand piano off to one side, and the crew and executives sat for most of the day in the bar/ restaurant area next to it debating how to navigate the unforeseen weather interruption. With little clue about what to expect from this experience I chose to remain in my hotel room reading while the rain persisted, unsure if making small talk with cameramen and art directors was the done thing in television. Besides I was having a phase of reading quite raunchy romance novels that opened up a sexual World to me I hadn't yet experienced in real life, and so reading was quite an exciting option. They checked in with me multiple times during the day and we always ate supper together at night. My big opportunity of starring in a UK TV commercial, a commercial I had resigned from my bank job to film, was falling apart at the seams, and eventually after seven days, three books and an extensive knowledge of the hotel gift shop we were informed that the entire cast and crew would be heading back to London and placed on hold while we waited out the weather. Again, in virgin territory I wasn't quite sure what a weather-hold meant. As it turns out it meant that I would be paid for 6 weeks as if I were filming every day. It was one of the biggest shocks of my early filming career. This was Coca-Cola after all, they had unlimited resources, and still to this day was the only time I had been flown anywhere First Class. I decided I would use this time during which I was not permitted to accept any other work as I would remain *on hold* to approach Model Agents in London *in person* and that fact is important to anyone seeking to break through in Entertainment. Though it may be *normal* to reach out and book appointments with agents and managers on the phone or online (*though good luck with that*) I always chose to simply *drop in* and say I was just passing by. I was seen 95% of the time using this tactic.

I decided to start at the top and work my way down, with my first drop-in being Model's One in World's End. Inside the room was full of male and female models who looked very much like they had been computer generated, almost too perfect. Some of the males were prettier than the females as this was the age of Androgyny and so the female models looked harder and more masculine while the boys were quite literally *beautiful.* I didn't look remotely like the female models that were lounging across the desks of their bookers. They didn't have curves like me, or long hair like me and they certainly didn't wear any make-up as I did. They looked more like a Punk Rock Ingrid Bergman with faces so scrubbed clean they were pink. I felt like I had arrived in the land of the giants and as I plodded my short self over to the desk feeling very much like a Hobbit I knew instinctively that they would never represent me. One of the male model bookers sitting at a desk surrounded by pretty boys was a girl who went on to become very famous indeed in the UK, her name was Davina McCall, and aside from a smile from her my welcome there was limited. I think they probably thought I was delivering sandwiches or something.

So undeterred I moved on to an agency called Storm. They represented Kate Moss, who, like me, wasn't so tall, so I thought I'd give it a shot. Their small boutique offices were extremely welcoming but the photographs on the walls of the models they represented were just not me. It was almost as if the photographers, models and make-up artists had conspired to make pretty girls look as awful as possible. Bright sunlight on near naked skin in extreme close-up showed every lash, every freckle and every line in their lips. To me it looked ugly as if someone had gone all out to *remove* or deliberately *dull* their beauty. I approached the desk and said to the girl,

I'm not right for you am I?

The receptionist shook her head gently as if to signal *don't bother.*
By now you may be realizing how rejection is very much part of modeling and acting. If you are the kind of personality who simply *gives up* when told *no* then don't bother with

entertainment. *The Push* as I call it, to gain *traction* in the business is unending and remains part of what you do for *Life*. My next agency was Elite Models London.

Known internationally but particularly in New York their models were a much wider range which spanned from *Girl Next Door* – a commercial type like me to *Supermodel* being the home of Cindy Crawford, Naomi Campbell & Christy Turlington. Theirs was a wall of faces, models and looks I could relate to. Unfortunately, though the models were definitely more like me the bookers at that time were not. They marched me into a luxurious bathroom and invited a 6ft tall Nigerian model in with us. She instructed us both to strip down to our underwear and pulled out a measuring tape. As I looked into the vast mirror in the cold, unforgiving bathroom lighting I saw what felt like Laurel & Hardy. The other model's body was long and lean, almost like a sculpture. Mine was that of an English girl next door.

She went on to measure her leg length then mine, her thigh width then mine, her waist then mine and her breast size then mine, before asking the Nigerian model to leave. Her address was cold and unforgiving.

She remarked,

You are too short (5'8"), too fat (120lbs), too old (19) and your boobs are too big (34B at the time).

My mouth dropped open. I asked.

How old was the girl who was just in here?

She replied,

Fourteen, and we wish we'd got to her sooner.

So now I knew I was out of my depth. It wasn't possible to grow younger and be 13 or 14 again, it was doubtful I would get any taller and I was already hovering at a weight so low for my height that my GP was getting concerned. And as for my boobs being too big? Wow, I'd always wanted them bigger!

She simply hated everything about me and I can only describe the look on her face as I stood there exposed in my underwear as a *Grimace*.

I left knowing that without the big three agencies my only options were going to be those not known on the World stage, which would be limiting.

I then hoofed my rejected arse over to Sloan Square and walked into *Freddie's*.

Up to that point I hadn't told any of the agents that I was the new face of Sprite and currently on a weather hold for Coca-Cola to return back to Lake Garda in Italy. I realized that as my options for representation began dwindling it might be something I should mention. As I walked into the small office containing a black oval shaped booking table with four people around it the reception I received was vastly different than anywhere else. A red headed lady (*Freddie*) pushed back her chair and stared at me as I entered. She glanced a look to the other agents that betrayed her interest in me and they raised their eyebrows.

Without mentioning the TV campaign, she made me feel wanted and valuable. She talked at length about getting my *book* together and began showing me photographs taken on test shoots with other models she had represented and they were great. I waited until the end, until she said *Okay then let's get you working!* before giving her the good news that her latest signing was already the face of the latest advertising campaign from the largest drink's manufacturer in the World. Coca-Cola was *Freddie's* good Karma because she gave a new face a chance that day.

My relationship with Freddie's went on to be very fruitful for all of us. I shot a multitude of campaigns for both television and print, the most notable being Lingerie shoots for Marks & Spencer. You see the types of ladies shopping in those stores didn't want to see supermodels in their knickers, they wanted to see someone who looked more like them, a girl with hips, tits and who looked like she had eaten that week. Unfathomably the smaller less *International* Model Agents were more *woke* in the nineties than the World-famous names. Freddies and their clients knew even then that *real women* sell in far greater numbers than unattainable ideals. Chanel may sell 500 bespoke suits thanks to a lithe teenage Supermodel, caught in her prime barely post puberty, but a pair of Marks & Sparks knickers on a curvaceous woman can run into hundreds of thousands of numbers retail. I discovered the modeling *underbelly,* the *meat.* It might not have been as visually glamorous as a ritzy Vogue shoot in Saint Tropez but by God it brought the cash in. Then, about a year later, when walking through Covent Garden on my way to a casting I bumped into the Elite Models booker who had hauled me into the bathroom with the Nigerian model. Her approach this time was staggeringly different, running at me as if having seen a long-lost friend.

Nicola darling girl! You are doing so well! All over TV and just killing it honey! Listen, I made a mistake, we want you at Elite. We want you as one of our girls.

I looked across the street at the large contemporary black frontage of Elite Models London. Giant poster prints of the Worlds most stunning supermodels hung at the windows. I knew instantly that her fawning was fake, that she was in fact that quite unpleasant, unwelcoming individual that had tried to humiliate me in a poorly lit bathroom a year earlier, but my business brain told me that it was my own achievements and determination that had brought me to this point, a place where the Worlds No.1 would beg in the street to represent me, and so I made a business decision, based in no way on how I felt about her personally.

I said,

I'm commercial. I like to make a lot of money. Can you bring that?

She shrieked and said,

Oh fuck yes!

And just like that I became Nicola Charles of Elite Model Management. TV & print campaigns followed for Ford Cars, Sunkisk, Oil of Olay, L'Oreal, Rimmel, Palmolive, Pantene, Schwartzkopt, Thomas Cook holidays, Haagen-Daz, Elizabeth Shaw chocolates, Lambs Navy Rum, Marks & Spencer, Freemans Catalogues, Ritter Sport Germany and many more as I flew around the Globe as what was surely Elites top *non-supermodel* raking in commercial pounds.

From that point on my life became quite lonely. I spent specific and structured amounts of time in different territories as Elite worked out how to make sure I wasn't *over-exposed*. I remember watching TV in London one night and of the five TV commercials in one single ad break I was in four of them. The phone rang ominously about 2 minutes after the ad break had aired and my booker said *Darling you need to go to Germany, there's too much of you here.* I lived and worked in Miami, Paris, Hamburg, Munich, Barcelona, Bermuda, Athens, London, Istanbul and Bahrain among others, and airport gates, hotels and model apartments became my homes, as I worked to make sure no single territory ever had *too much* of me. I would spend certain seasons in certain territories, one of the most lucrative financially being the season for shooting German Fashion Catalogues that required me to live and work in Miami, Florida for about two months of every year.

(PHOTO: Berlin, early nineties. It was strange to become a "local" in cities all over the World as I dropped in and out for a few months at a time.)

Staying in a Hotel adjacent to the News Café and not far from Versace's home on South Beach I would wait out the days until word came that a car would be collecting me to take me down to the Keys. I watched for weeks as women with perfect plastic surgery enhanced body's roller bladed along South Beach hoping to be spotted by a Donald Trump or other Billionaire type. I stayed inside, the news updates of drive-by shootings and robberies of pregnant women at ATM's absolutely terrifying me. On 15th July 1997 my worst Miami fears were confirmed, when less than half a mile from the hotel I used to stay at, Gianni Versace was shot and killed, right there on South Beach, at the gate to his own home.

Shoots would always take place at the beginning and end of the day for the purposes of lighting. The Sun you see is the most stunning of all lamps, hovering like a purpose-built warm lighting structure directly at the face both at sunrise and sunset, whilst being totally useless and causing under-eye shadows during the middle of the day. I would always be asked to be in the make-up chair in the make-up artists hotel room at around 4.30am to be on set by 6. While I was beautified the photographer and assistant would be on the beach setting up the shot, so that when the sweet spot of the sunrise was upon us, I would be leaning on a palm tree in a hideous German sweater and bare tanned legs with Cindy

Crawford hair *laughing hysterically* at a joke that had never been told. I knew what I was doing and I was quick, and it was the reason I earned the big money. Photographers didn't need to coach me into *looking natural* or *making love to the camera* I just instinctively knew it. We'd always be done by 8.30am when the light became harsher, having motored through a rail of equally hideous clothing, and then the day was my own. I had cars, drivers and cash *per diem (an allowance given each day)* and a plethora of Miami stores to cruise around. I got to know many countries pretty well, all while living first class on client's money, the USA, France, Germany, Spain, Italy, Bahrain, Australia, Morocco, Greece, Turkey and more. But for all the perceived glamour of my lifestyle I was alone with my thoughts a lot. I had a model boyfriend back home in England who didn't seem to miss me that much, a Mother who barely stayed in touch, an absent father and no time to make friends, so I began befriending stray animals at almost every location I was sent, spending my days sunbathing, which wasn't really allowed, and feeding the stray cats and dogs. On TV or inside catalogues I looked like the girl who had the most glamorous life imaginable. A girl who surely left the photo shoot and ran into the arms of a Billionaire boyfriend who would wine and dine her at restaurants around the globe, but the sad truth is that once the client had their fake-happy shots to sell their hideous clothing I became incredibly dispensable. The thing I struggled with most was the knowledge that as a *model* no-one was remotely interested in anything I had to say, and if I did ever try and start a conversation on literally any subject matter, I would often get comments like *Where did that come from? We're not paying you to think?* For a number of years, I would muse on how I got there from banking and if I had made the right choice, especially as this new career had a shelf life. What did stand out though was my ability to learn scripts for TV commercials and perform the scenarios naturally and effortlessly for camera, over and over and over again. No mistakes, no fluffed lines, no loss of energy during takes. Then one day a very famous hairdresser in London called Sam brushed my hair between takes for the L'Oreal Pumping Curls campaign and whispered something in my ear.

You're an actress darling not a model. Get a theatrical agent.

He provocatively drew the long hair he had just brushed through his fingers and eyeballed me as he walked away raising his eyebrows and winking. Hearing it said out-loud was extremely empowering and inspiring. I was a model, but one who also liked to walk and talk, move around, be animated, create *Characters.*

Like, The girl who used the Worlds best shampoo or *The girl who drove the latest sporty hatchback from Ford* or *The girl was never going to age because she used Oil of Olay twice daily* or *The girl with remarkably white teeth despite downing endless gulps of soft drink* or *the girl who had the best sex life on earth because she ate a famous brand of ice-cream in the bath.*

Because when I was given a job to do, a role to play, a scenario to build, I climbed inside it, ran away from who I was, and lived the dream not just for pretend, but temporarily *for real.* Actresses are mad like that, its what makes us a slightly different breed. Here I had found my escape, I had found a way to not be Nicola Charles anymore, and each time I was handed a script I became like the childhood character I used to watch on TV. *Mr.Benn* would leave his house in Festive Road and try on costumes in a costume shop. Once dressed in the outfits he would walk through a door at the back of the costume shop and into the World of whichever character he was wearing and I was doing the same. I didn't wear glamorous clothing or drive glamorous cars. I didn't eat ice-cream in the bathtub or live my life with inexplicably shiny hair, but I happily would, if you paid me to.

Back home in England I bought myself my first car. It was a bright red Renault 5 Turbo. In hindsight it looked like a rather hideous jelly mold but at the time it felt extremely fancy indeed. I drove it home with my boyfriend in the passenger seat and displaying L-plates. I was 20 years old but hadn't passed my driving test yet. I'd been hooning around some private land in my boyfriend's father's rather dilapidated 1961 Land Rover 110. It hadn't seen an MOT in years and in order to drive in a straight line you had to jiggle the steering wheel wildly from ten to two and changing gear was extremely violent indeed. I bounced around inside the cab as if on bedsprings, often hitting my head on the roof as I flew over potholes and down muddy ditches in the massive aluminum truck. I developed a soft spot for the old girl and though I didn't know it at the time it was something that would stay with me for life. I guess you could say she was my *first,* and a lady never forgets her *first.*

By contrast the Renault was like driving a formula one car, and while many females I knew were expecting the men in their lives to purchase a car for them, I was proudly buying my own. I was living in Surrey at the time. Well, when I say living, I mean the place I stayed during the short periods I wasn't working overseas. The inside of the Renault smelt like nothing I had inhaled before. Something about the new car smell made me want to speed! The car was primarily designed for rallying and when the street model came out it exceeded all expectations. My hot hatch had a four-cylinder turbo charged engine with a top speed of 200kph. I can tell you now that the boring route up the A3 from Guildford to London in my boyfriends Fiat126 was boring no more! I had passed my test 1st time while my little red machine was waiting patiently in the garage for me to take control of her and I wasted no time. When I finally did get behind the wheel of my own car, I lost all sense of responsibility and caution and drove that girl like I'd stolen her.

One appointment required me to travel up through Enfield in North London. I had never had to navigate their one-way systems before and during an era prior to Google Maps I was reading road signs whilst travelling at 50mph. It was mid-morning and the traffic was light, in fact on my stretch of the one-way system the road was completely empty. The road had three lanes on either side with a large metal crash barrier standing at about 10 feet tall between the two sides, meaning that traffic travelling in the other direction wasn't visible. I guess that may be why a sleepy Butcher in a van carrying carcasses of beef around London entered my side of the one-way system believing it was a two-way deal. Still doing 50mph in the far-right lane and having had my driving license for approximately eight weeks, I watched on in horror as the van entered from a side road to my left ahead of me, and swung right to face me in the fast lane. I had absolutely no time to think and pulled my foot off the accelerator instinctively swerving left *sadly at the same time he did* slamming my foot down on the brake pedal. But I was 20 years old and in a very small fast car. You see, I didn't actually hit the brake pedal at all, I had hit the accelerator again and was only aware of that fact when a high-pitched whistling noise filled the cabin and became the last thing I heard before impact. I had just engaged the Turbo and in slow motion my little car seemed to now fly like a heat-seeking missile directly into the now swerving van.

When the Police arrived, they had to forcibly remove my foot from the accelerator and only then did the intense whirring of the engine finally end. Luckily the only thing that died that day was my Renault 5 Turbo. The van driver had a broken shoulder and we had both just had the luckiest escape of our lives.

Four weeks later my insurance company sent me the value of my now scrapped Renault 5 Turbo so I could buy a new car. I went to the wreckers yard to take one last look at her and do her the honor of saying goodbye. The front was squashed up like the face of a British Bulldog with the damage encroaching only slightly on the cabin, these were the days before crumple zones and plastic cars, but any more and it would have been curtains for me. I thought about all the times I had taken chances with my life as a kid, all the risks and all the near misses, telling myself I didn't care about my own life, but in that moment, I realized I wasn't ready to die and still felt there must be some purpose to surviving this, so I went straight down to Land Rover in Dorking and bought a second-hand Land Rover 90, which the sales guy told me wouldn't be able to get past 70mph on Motorways. I decided then and there that despite having been raised around speed and racing as a child, fast cars were not for me. My crash headache lasted for about two weeks.

So with rich men and fast cars off the table, what else did life have in store for me?

3

In 1991 I was working consistently as a model and doing very well financially. There was no need to do test shoots for photography for my *Portfolio* known as my *Book* but as a predominantly commercial model I felt it might be prudent to do some so that my looks inside it were up to date. Two of my favorite photographers to work with at the time were John Swannell and Tony McGee. John was a classic old-school photographer. He spent his time photographing Royalty and became well known for his beautiful depictions of Princess Diana. However, the majority of my work with John was nudes. This I found interesting because I did not have a traditionally skinny, boney model figure and yet he captured something so *Woman* about me I found it very difficult to say no to him. In fact, it was the ease with which I shot nudes with John that gave me the confidence when asked to shoot for The Joy of Sex book in the UK around the same time. A handful of shots were taken of myself and my partner, also a professional model at the time, in faux sexual positions, for what turned out to be a surprisingly arty photo shoot. Our heads were chopped off so no-one would ever know it was us and the shoot consisted of just us two and the female photographer. Throughout my entire television career, I lived in fear that those photographs, though completely innocent, would appear *with heads attached* and out me for accepting the job in the press, thus damaging my image whilst on a G rated television show. It never happened and I would like to thank The Joy of Sex for that.

By contrast my shoots with Tony McGee, arranged so that both of us could benefit from the use of his photographs, were for me at the time highly editorial in nature. In other words, photographs that could easily grace the pages of glossy fashion magazines, except they wouldn't, because the model in question, *me*, was too *commercial* and in fashion *that* is unforgivable. His shots captured a moment in time for me that can never be re-lived. His direction while shooting, which was quite pushy and flirty in nature, brought out a spark in my eyes that very few ever captured, and of all the photo shoots contained in my *Book* they are the ones that still get the most compliments to this day. And so after a couple of years of shooting together Tony asked me to be one of three models to travel to Australia with him to shoot the *Lamb's Navy Rum*

Calendar. The Calendar was titled *Latitude 21,* which of course is Australia, and ironically, I was also 21 at the time. I had traveled almost everywhere in the World at that point but had never been as far as Australia. This trip altered the course of my life permanently.

I had never flown anywhere for 28 hours or needed a stop over for a 747 Jumbo Jet to *refuel* to get there! It was exciting and new and armed with my CD Walkman which contained just one CD *the self titled album by SEAL* I packed a capsule wardrobe of model essentials like vests, shorts and track pants, wore my trusty Birkenstocks *a must for any self-respecting model or make-up artist working in the hottest countries in the World* and let my Australian adventure begin. I remember the moment our plane reached what must have been the North Western corner of Australia and the pilot telling us to look down as the stunning coastline came into view. Its beauty was staggering as the deep blue waters topped off with white surf rippled along a golden and heat scorched coastline, it was like nothing I had ever seen before and it took my breath away. I remembered childhood, and how my Dad had always begged my Mother to move as a family to Australia, and she had always said no. I leant my head against the tiny plane window as I gazed down at the mighty Australia and mouthed words to my Father in the hopes that wherever he was he might hear me.

I made it Dad

To my complete surprise the plane did not start its descent, in fact it continued its flight path over Australia for hours and hours. *Wow!* I thought *how big is this place?????*

Eventually we began our descent into Sydney airport. It was late January and as I walked from the cabin into the tunnel to the gate, I began to feel the unique heat of Australia filtering in. When we had left London Heathrow, there had been snow on the ground and spending any amount of time outside was literally painful it was so cold, but here, down under, there were no such problems, and it felt like I had arrived in a pre-historic land, unlike anywhere else I had ever been. There were many odors in the air that day, suntan oil, sweat, hot bodies and the unmistakable scent of hope. It was all around me, and though my *home* was literally on the other side of the

World I felt there was a very big reason I had ended up in this place.

The Australian accents were fantastic and hysterical, and the Aussies I encountered seemed to feel the same way about mine when I spoke. I hadn't realized that Aussie's *really do* say things like *Strewth* and *Bastard* routinely. Along with a whole host of other choice words generally used and I very much admired the freedom with which Australian's spoke their truth and still do, although sadly these days the authenticity of that has been watered down by Political Correctness.

After collecting our luggage, we headed outside to the waiting bus that would take us to our hotel and as the doors of the terminal opened late afternoon in Sydney the heat hit me like a truck, only in Bahrain had I experienced anything like it, and it was wondrous. Forget England's green and pleasant land I thought, I would happily take this heat-scorched place over freezing to death any day of the week. We had one night at a Sydney hotel before catching a flight the next day to Alice Springs, and if I thought Sydney was hot, I could never have imagined what 48 degrees Celsius would feel like, or should I say for those in England 118.4 degrees Fahrenheit! A literal *WALL* of heat engulfed me at Alice Springs and as it did, I could actually feel my body consciously thinking *Easy now this could kill us.* Unusual things began happening to my skin as it bristled with what felt like tiny pin pricks along my arms and face. My ankles were beginning to swell up and simply breathing took on a whole new dimension as it was something I needed to now *think about* and not just do as a reflex. *This* I thought *is a serious place. This* is somewhere humans are not supposed to be. I wondered how food could be transported, stored and kept here, how enough water for everybody could ever be collected or how *anyone* could work a normal job in *this?*

We were taken swiftly to an Executive mini-bus, that belted out air-conditioning like Santa's hair-dryer and I was so very grateful for it. Similarly, the foyer of the Hotel we arrived at in Alice Springs was also pumping out the air-con as if power and energy were nothing to be concerned about. As we gathered our vast luggage for check-in, I could see through a central glass wall a pool area with a circle of empty sun loungers surrounding it, all clearly scorched by a Sun that had the strength to destroy furniture. I was not surprised at all that no people were silly enough to be out there and I began praying that power failures were not a regular occurrence in Australia.

Call it luck or design I really don't know but the calendar months being shot for those two days in Alice Springs were with the two blonde models on our trip and I was given the time off to sight see. *Fuck that for a game of soldiers!* I told myself *I'm not leaving this hotel!* And I didn't. I remember more than a little resentment that night at dinner as two rather pissed-off blondes came down to eat with the photographic crew and made it very clear they hadn't appreciated my time off. One launched a rather bitchy attack on my being a vegetarian at the time and said that only stupid people would choose to be put off eating meat by videos of slaughter houses that had been shown to me by Animal Rights groups. I didn't bite back; I knew my vegetarianism wasn't the issue that night it was the luxury I had been afforded to watch TV in an air-conditioned hotel room all day. As we walked the halls back to our rooms after dinner one of them approached me and said,

If you want any coaching on how to move in front of camera let me know, so you're not quite so limited.

I thanked her graciously and popped the keycard in my hotel room door before falling about laughing on the bed. I never let her poor attitude put me off people from Wisconsin but I will also never forget her Princess attitude after being made to walk twenty minutes through an Australian gorge to reach the background scenery for her shot, and then being expected to look good on a forty-eight-degree day.

Next, we headed to Mount Isa.

If I punch Mount Isa into Google Maps from Melbourne it tells me that if *driving* it will take me 19 days and 14 hours to get there, such is the vastness of Australia. The town became famous in the World of mining for holding the largest deposits of Lead, Silver, Copper and Zinc ever discovered, anywhere in the World. I was unaware of that history at the time, and having been advised by a local that it was merely a central town where Post got sorted, I discovered for myself another inescapable and extremely painful fact. That being, that Mount

Isa is home to possibly the largest and most terrifying Mosquitoes I have ever had the misfortune to meet.

It was night one in Mount Isa when I lay my head down to sleep in the humble Motel accommodation we were staying in. I had spent the day being photographed with a Cowgirl on her Horse who was apparently the local Rodeo Champion. I was looking forward to some well-earned rest and knew that with the absence of air-conditioning in this particular Motel it wouldn't be easy.

With the windows wide open and protected by fly-screens I began to slowly drift off. Somewhere between sleep and awake I heard a familiar and unpleasant humming sound. I began scratching at my face, shoulder and ankles furiously. It couldn't be a Mosquito as all the windows had screens on them. Then the humming sound seemed to land on my ear, and all at once an entire side of my head felt hot and itchy. My eyes zeroed in on the fly screen near the kitchen area, where there, previously unseen was a giant hole in the screen about the size of a fifty-cent piece, big enough for a Huntsman Spider to crawl through never mind a Mosquito! Now, I realize you are probably thinking *What's the big deal, we all get bitten by Mosquitoes,* well the big deal is this, up to this point I'd had no idea that I would be chronically allergic to Australian Mosquitoes. I had been bitten in Spain, Miami and Greece, but had never seen anything more than a small bite, but as I ran to the light switch in the room and gazed upon the carnage of my body in the mirror, I was well aware that these were no ordinary Mosquitoes. My face, due to be photographed the following day no longer resembled the one I had arrived with. Instead, one half of it distinctly resembled E.T. Yes, E.T. the Extra-terrestrial. My cheekbone looked as if I had gone five rounds with Mike Tyson, and my corresponding eye socket looked the same. On the other side my ear was larger than normal and bright red, and from top to toe I could see massive swellings about the size of golf balls everywhere, approximately forty of them. I ran for the Make-up Artists room in tears hoping she'd have some kind of ointment to help as the skin on my face began feeling tighter and tighter as the swelling continued, but as her initial reaction was one you'd expect of someone who had just seen the Elephant Man *sans hood* I knew the situation was serious. She made some calls, and quite soon the entire crew, along with the two bitchy blondes, one from London the other from

Wisconsin stood around in disbelief at the *new Nicola* that sat on the end of the bed before them scratching furiously. Shortly afterwards a *Bush Doctor* arrived. She was a large, jolly woman who picked my problem immediately.

You're one of those VEGETARIANS are you? She quipped.

It seems that bush Mosquitoes are a little bit partial to a Vegetarian. I learned that day that meat sours the blood, and Mosquitoes absolutely love sweet blood.

These bad boys would've been able to smell a Vegetarian from 70 kilometers away! Don't get many in these parts. She went on.

The model from Wisconsin smirked as her fingers rested daintily over her mouth, unable to resist feasting her eyes on the horror that sat before her. The bush doctor asked everyone to leave the room before administering a large injection of Vitamin B into my bottom, enough I was told to sour my blood sufficiently that I may be able to leave the area alive. She instructed the photographer that my swelling would need

24-48 hours to go down at best, and gave me some anti-inflammatory tablets along with antihistamines.

I began to wonder if my Australian adventure was quite for me after all as the photographer rolled his eyes in disbelief. The heat, the mosquitoes and lack of good vegetarian food were starting to take their toll and now I was unable to work. I had become the problem child of the shoot and so I sheepishly apologized and made my way back to my room, where I found motel staff spraying enough insect repellent to fell an elephant and another hastily replacing the fly screen. When everyone left, I closed every window, covered my entire body in calamine lotion and lay down in agony on the floor amidst a sea of wet towels and toxic air almost too thick with insect repellent to breath, to ease the pain of the bites, and looked forward to the next day which would see us begin our journey to Ayers Rock at Australia's *Red Centre*.

Sacred to Indigenous Australian's Ayers Rock is thought to have started forming 550 Million years ago and as we trekked through the outback in two 4x4's to get there I certainly felt a spirituality all around that I hadn't expected. The ground beneath the trucks turned slowly from Salt Flats that created mirages all around us, mirages that always seemed so ironic, always displaying what looked like Lakes of glittering water amidst the dryness, to a thick, deep red dust that covered the vehicles in a layer of what resembled clay which choked up the air-conditioning as we powered along the desert tracks for hour upon hour.

When I delve into my memory banks and think about one of the incredible sights along our journey, The Olga's, that's when I know a small part of me must be insane because the very clear memory I have of the Olga's is that they were giant black balls of rock piled up on top of each other like rabbit droppings. When in reality, the Olga's are a large red domed rock formation that look more like the bombardments of a Castle, not like rabbit droppings at all. Perhaps the many days of heat and driving had somehow skewed my memory of it, perhaps seeing such an incredible sight at such a young age brought it to me with an unusual perspective, or perhaps like my father I simply chose to see something in my head a certain way, and therefore my brain made it fact.

A shot was taken of me that I still have framed on the wall of my house today. Ayers Rock in the back ground, an old 1950's Ute parked in front, leant on by a smoldering cowboy meant to be my lover, and me, naked all but a dirty old shirt and wellington boots *Gum boots Australians would say,* about to lift a giant log of driftwood as I stare longingly back towards the truck, an Australian Kelpie dog at my side. I have to say, after getting my head into the mindset that I *did* in fact live on a Cattle Station in the middle of the Australian bush, playing the role was a doddle. And let's face it compared to sitting on a chilly train that stopped at every station between Worcestershire and Birmingham New Street station, it was a much more interesting way to earn a living. The photographer proudly showed the shots around that night at dinner to the other models and crew as they sat down for a meal of Kangaroo Steaks and I once again asked for anything that contained Tomato.

That night the other models decided that my new nickname was *Tomato* and I was referred to as such for the remainder of the trip. I didn't mind, I somehow understood it was punishment for not having to shoot at Alice Springs in 48-

degree heat, and when the girl from Wisconsin began making noises of enjoyment as she chomped on her Kangaroo steak, oil leaking from the sides of her mouth as she said *I just love living in ignorance, this steak is so damn good* I knew I was right about her. I could see from the window a mob of Kangaroos outside, males, females and young all hanging out together in the vastness of the Australian bush, and I told myself that living in ignorance would never be something I would choose to do.

Our next stop would be Walkabout Greek.

Made famous by the Australian blockbuster movie *Crocodile Dundee* Walkabout Creek and the Walkabout Creek Hotel are crammed full of memorabilia from the movie. It simply doesn't get any more Australian. I remember sitting out the front with a cold drink marveling at the nothingness of the location when everything started shaking, like an Earthquake was beginning. The man from the hotel came out drying his hands on a tea towel and said,

Road Train coming through.

The rumbling went on for a couple of minutes before in the distance I could see the glinting of Sun bouncing off metal as something massive this-way-came. Like a scene from Mad Max an enormous truck, one that seemed twice as large as regular trucks approached and really didn't slow down at all. The man from the hotel spoke again.

Don't step out now, stay right where you are, those things take about a mile to stop. Too heavy to brake for anything or anyone that gets in the way.

After what felt like another five or so minutes of rumbling the enormous *Road Train* was passing by us. Though the multiple trailers being pulled no doubt contained products, food and post destined for the opposite end of the country, in my highly imaginative young mind they were Circus trailers, and as each one passed by, I saw first the Lions, then a Giraffes head sticking out of the top of the cage and finally the Elephants through the wooden side doors of a vintage carriage designed for the purpose. I sat there immersed in the dust it left behind and giggled to myself about the fantasy of animal friends I had just had. You see my ability to transport myself into that

World, into any World, had always been a pocket of myself I was able to access at any time. It had indeed begun on that floor behind the couch when I was five years old when my next-door-neighbour had shoved a Chupa-Chup lollypop down my throat to stop me screaming as he sexually assaulted me. *That* had been my first go at an out of body experience. It worked brilliantly as I floated up out of myself and watched the horror of what was happening from the vantage point of the ceiling, as far away from the man as possible. Removing my soul meant that in the moment I felt no pain, and though I am not in any way religious, I will always know for sure that a force, which cannot be explained or catalogued by us saved me that day. I always used to wonder if this ability was available to everyone, and almost hoped it would be, for those who were taken and murdered. I had prayed they were able to separate from it, and have lived every day since reasonably sure they could.

And so as I sat there the photographer approached me followed closely by what looked like a cowboy. The cowboy resembled Tom Cruise, which was odd, and years later I would wonder if he really did, or if I had imagined that too, but the photographic evidence, which remains to this day, confirms it.

This is Paul. He works on the Cattle Station and he's going to be in tomorrows shot.

I looked at this *real person* that had been brought in to add a touch of authenticity to my shoot and as the photographer walked away leaving us together, I felt an uneasy sense of inevitability from both of them. Inevitability of what I wasn't quite sure. The cowboy sat next to me on the rickety wooden bench and stared out into the vastness of the bush.

You'll have to help me I have no idea what I'm doing.

The stranger was talking to me and at 21 going on 15 I had no idea what to say to him.

Why are you doing it then? I asked naively.

Same reason you are I guess, money. They offered it to me. He replied.

Suddenly I felt sympathy for him. We were both just pawns of the machine. Both sat there on that desolate bench in the middle of the Australian bush waiting to have our youngness photographed and gazed upon by Lord knows whom for cold hard cash. I smiled at him and threw him a rope.

That's okay. It's easy. Just pretend we know each other and it will look good. He's a great photographer.

The next morning at dawn when the biggest Sun I had ever seen began breaking with it's threatened heat of the day on the horizon I emerged from the Hair & Make-up artists room with big hair, sun-tanned make-up on my already sun-tanned skin and a playsuit that was unbuttoned enough for one breast to fall out. This was a calendar shoot for rum after all, not Woman's Own. In front of the Walkabout Creek Hotel, which in itself looked like a movie set, hence it was used as one, had been placed a small metal table and two metal chairs. Adjacent was a wooden rail used to tie up horses and leaning on it was *Paul* the Tom Cruise lookalike Cattle Ranger holding a beer at 6am in a stubby holder *a foam cup holder designed to keep beers cold in 40-degree heat.* I too was handed a beer in a stubby holder and told to sit down.

Moments later a man appeared holding a Blue Healer dog, an Australian Cattle dog known for snapping at the heals of cows to move them along, and he placed the dog onto the metal table where it curled up happily watching for movement in the vast nothingness and sticking the tip of it's tongue out to stay cool. The stage was set, the cute cowboy and his sexually charged girlfriend were taking a break from bush life to sit for a beer in the searing heat of an Australian day. The shot was a triumph and I love it to this day, but I will always remember how Paul got a little too lost in the fake World we had created for a photograph and began to believe that he and I were somehow girlfriend and boyfriend for real.

That night, as we sat at dinner with the crew and other models, Paul arrived with a friend to join us for drinks. His friend seemed to know the barman very well and so spent the night chatting with him, while Paul was focused very strongly on his new girlfriend, *me*. The other models and crew seemed to be in on the set-up and it almost felt as if I had been sold to this boy from a cattle station at Walkabout Creek without being consulted. He stayed around as the others slowly petered off and went to their rooms and suddenly, we were alone as his friend waved him goodbye. It was only a short distance of about 60 meters to my room but I knew that once I had made the decision to go this stranger was going to try and come with me. He asked me if he could show me his Ute outside. I had no idea what a Ute was, and fearful of what might come next, I said.

Okay but then I have to go to bed we're leaving tomorrow.

I could see the fear in his eyes, pain almost, that he only had that night to impress me, to do or say *anything* that would make me give up my life as an international model and stay here in this desert place with him until the end of time. The polite English side of me began kicking in, a side I have worked hard to beat out of existence for many years, the people pleaser side, and I was seriously unhappy about what was happening. This was the inevitability I had felt, this was what the cast and crew of the shoot and this stranger had all decided was going to happen, that Nicola Charles was going to get laid, and I had to think quickly to stop it.

We stood next to his canary yellow Ute with some kind of plastic canopy on the back that looked as though it might hold dogs for travel. A tank of water was sitting on the top of it with tubes hanging out. He must have seen me looking at it because he went on to explain at length that it was his *bush shower* for the times he was spending so long in the field he couldn't come in for washes and would shower out there in the vastness of the dry earth among his cattle. Suddenly with a click he had opened up the back and I half expected three German Shepherds to jump out. Inside were blankets and an old looking green sleeping bag, which he told me was called *A Swag*. It really was a turning point moment for me, I began to panic and realizing there must surely be only one reason he was showing me this turned back to him to tell him I was heading to my room. As I turned, I came face to face with a boy naked from the waist down. My model boyfriend back home, who never seemed to miss me and was reasonably self-absorbed had been a little challenged in the *Man Dept.* I'd realized that without having much experience of men at all, but now, in the cold blue light of the moon, as I stared in shock at this Australian giant penis, I was 100% sure that my boyfriend at home must be suffering from some hideous growth suppression disease. Paul's penis was as large and erect as I ever thought one might get and his face betrayed a longing that made me almost want to take pity on him. *A mercy fuck? Omg no, no, no.* You see at 21 I simply wasn't a sexual being. It didn't drive me, it didn't seem alive in me, and I simply didn't care whether I was sexual or not.

Sometimes I have told myself it was the abuse, but really, I think in part I was simply a very late developer. In fact, I was not a sexual being in the ways I fantasized wanting to be, until well into my forties.

I waited patiently for the magic to arrive. The magic that removed me from painful situations and took me somewhere else, somewhere safe, but it never came. Instead, I was face to face with Paul's lust and I was going to have to deal with it like a grown-up, despite feeling giant helpings of childlike fear. I took a deep breath and spoke as he looked on like a lovesick puppy, every fiber of his being longing to be with me.

It's very nice. But I'm sorry, I can't. I have a boyfriend at home.

I felt I had been more than generous considering this boy had assumed completely that I was a sure thing. Shockingly he spoke back without pulling his pants up.

Do you love him? Because I reckon I love you.

The look of confusion on my face didn't seem to dull his intensity. Did this boy from the cattle station really believe he loved me? Or that I could love him? After taking one photograph together?

Please just touch it. He asked.

3-2-1 and suddenly I was back in the room of my childhood neighbour, my head began to spin, I was five years old again and lying helpless behind my next-door neighbours couch with his hands all over me, rubbing my non-existent breasts and breathing his gross adult breath on me. My PTSD had kicked in and I had two options, flight or fight. If flight was my ability to transport my soul away from this danger then it wasn't kicking in down here in Australia, and so I had to fight, metaphorically, by using my strongest grown-up words.

No I won't touch it. I won't be doing anything with it. Please find some nice Australian girl to be with, someone who actually loves you.

Finally, he pulled his pants up as best he could over his huge erection and took a breath.

I knew I wouldn't be able to make it happen. I just thought that maybe, if you slept with me, and realized what I felt for you, you'd know. He said.

So I spoke the words I would use to all those making advances to me during work time overseas and I was very proud of myself as a woman when I said them.

I am here to WORK not fall in Love.

And with that I took a deep breath and walked off to my room, hoping and praying with every step that the horny Australian cattle rancher wouldn't grab me from behind or take this to a place we could never come back from. My hands shook violently as I fumbled the key into the wobbly lock of the door to my room, a door that felt like it was made of cardboard and would surely be incapable of stopping anything. But I never saw Paul again, he wasn't there the next morning as we packed up our large amounts of luggage into our two 4x4's, I never saw his yellow Ute at the Hotel or on the road out of town and the barman who seemed to know Paul looked at me as if I must be a stuck-up bitch for not wanting to sleep with a *real man.* I won't ever forget Paul. I don't think of him as a predator or someone I needed to be afraid of, I just remember him as a horny boy who made many assumptions about me because he didn't have time to find out who I really was. And let's face it, some men can spend years with us and still not truly know *who* we are, so one night of passion was never going to cut it. Now I'm older I do often look at the photograph and wonder if I would have changed course after a night with Paul. Part of me wishes I could've prevented what came next in my life by staying at Walkabout Creek forever, isn't hindsight a wonderful thing.

Our second to last stop was truly epic.

THE GREAT BARRIER REEF!

How could I ever describe to you the wonder and beauty of the Great Barrier Reef? I have not enough talent in my fingertips to do its majesty justice. Our base was on Hamilton Island. The hotel pool had a bar in the center you needed to swim out to, and little golf karts took you the short distances from one beach to another or between shopping areas. Giant Fruit Bats hung like black wet leaves from the surrounding trees, only moving at night, and in the waters just off the sands could be seen shoals of fish zigzagging just beneath the crystal-clear waters. Everyone on the island had an island mentality and nothing was too much trouble, and they did all they could to ensure we would always want to come back. We weren't shooting until the next day and so I decided to go for a swim and relax a little. I've always been able to open my eyes under water even in the ocean and without a mask or goggles so was able to look at the sea life just beneath the surface. Some of the fish were the size of dinner plates, and fat like large goldfish. Some of those were *see through!* And I could see their organs pulsating as they swam. I hadn't even gone out far enough to lose the sand beneath my feet and yet I was totally surrounded by fish. It felt a little unsettling as I had only seen this kind of thing on footage of Piranha fish attacking humans in documentaries, as they swam and swerved all around me. I looked out into the vast blue openness and wondered, wow, what must be out there in the deep? Suddenly my foot stood on something squishy beneath the sand. I looked down realizing I had stood on something that had been resting down there and in my blurred vision mis-identified it as a Manta Ray. My mind got lost in the romance of divers I had seen in documentaries holding onto the shoulders of Manta Rays and being pulled along. I strained my eyes to see if the underneath was white but the creature had kicked up quite a lot of sand and I couldn't clearly see. I heard a loud and distant sound from somewhere above me, was it screaming? But carried on trying to grab the shoulders of the beast as it thrashed around, unhappy about being disturbed. As I pushed forward to do so, my leg was suddenly *stroked* by what felt like a barbed tail. My instincts flung me back and I bobbed up to the surface to see a man swimming at me furiously yelling,

Don't touch that! It's a Sting Ray!

I guess I had naively imagined this place was like a theme park, or some carefully managed aquarium, and that close encounters with deadly sea-life would be almost impossible. I was wrong! I swam back to the beach with the life-guard who sat me down for a brief history of the Great Barrier Reef, along with a stern warning about not swimming or diving alone.

Feeling more than a little foolish I headed over to the pool bar and decided a stiff drink was in order after what was explained had been a lucky escape. The other two models on our trip were seated in expensive looking bikinis flirting outrageously with the barman and loudly telling him in great detail about their international careers as top models. I dove under the surface to wash the salt water from my hair and popped up next to them unexpectedly amid looks of disapproval that I was wearing a very old day-glow orange bikini that had seen better days. I ordered a Vodka-Lime and soda. The barman said,

Wow you look like a Mermaid under the water with your long hair.

The model from Wisconsin chimed in,

OMG your eyes are so red, and you're DRINKING? Alcohol?

I turned to look at her, blonde blow-dry somehow intact despite making the short swim over to the bar in deep water, judgment written all over her face and said,

You know what, one of these days you're going to stop worrying about what I do so much.

And I slugged my drink and swam away.
The next morning we headed onto a 70ft sail boat being used for our shoot. The captain sailed her deep off Hayman Island as that would be the backdrop to the photo, and dropped anchor. My photo was up first and over with pretty quickly and once done I was told I was *free*. I could see something swimming rapidly along the side of the boat jumping up and down, very quickly, and tried desperately to photograph it with my Nikon. The Captain arrived next to me and told me it was a Sea Turtle. As a child I had a Tortoise called Molly. The Turtle looked exactly the same, only huge and fast!

You can dive in you know. The Captain said.

What? Really? Is it safe? I asked.

Yeah it's safe. I'll stay here and watch. They look pretty amazing when you see from under the water. Take a mask.

So I decided I would.

After all, we had just one day on the Yacht, and this was *The Great Barrier Reef* for God's sake! So I dove into the clear but dark waters to lay eyes upon the galloping sea turtle, and have the memory of it for life. I think I was in there for about five minutes searching with my eyes for the now vanished creature before something very unexpected happened. As I looked down into the blackness of the deep below, it seemed to be coming up. As if the ocean floor were rising. I felt instantly nauseous and thought perhaps I was having some kind of funny turn. This wasn't like the Sting Ray with blurry, blood shot eyes, this time I was wearing a mask, and the movement was very clear. I began to tread water slowly and was too afraid to go back to the surface only six feet above me, for fear of taking my eyes off the sight beneath. Then I realized what I was looking at, and it was looking at me.

My heart began racing like never before, think 100 coffees on an empty stomach, I pushed up to the surface for air gasping in shock, half wanting to scream, half believing this was the end of everything as life suddenly felt like a scene from a scary movie. I briefly saw the Captain pointing and smiling, which told me all was okay and so I pushed back down with my head to make sure, and yep, there it was, a goddamned Whale looking at me. I won't lie I shit my pants, not literally, but almost. It was half as long as the boat and twice as majestic. It had swum up to take a look at us, me or the boat I can't know, but it was definitely getting an eyeful. It's amazing the thoughts that run through your head in a moment like that, the brain going through its checklists.

Do whales bite humans?

Do whales eat humans?

Do whales use their tails to kill humans?

And while the checklist was going it suddenly turned on a sixpence faster than a London cab swinging round for a fare and rushed back down to the deep, the force of its exit causing a massive undercurrent that almost pulled me down. Holy

Christ and Mother of Jesus I was a changed woman. I swam up and over to the ladder where a very happy and excited Captain was waiting, as promised.

Did you see her? What a beauty! I think she was checking you out! He laughed.

I climbed out silently, in shock, in awe, in relief, that I had made it out alive. All the while glancing back down at the waters, just in case she chased me out, Jaws style!
The captain threw a towel around me and smiled.

Now you know. Now you know don't you! Welcome to Straya!

He said, as he wandered off back down the boat grinning from ear to ear, knowing this little girl from England would never forget that day.

(PHOTO: The Great Barrier Reef. Named so, because well, it is extremely great. There are no words to describe something nature put there. It isn't man-made and cannot be adequately man-described. It has a strange ability to make you realize you are insignificant and yet blessed to see it all at the same time.)

I stood there panting, dripping wet, knowing that living on land, is definitely where humans are supposed to be.

I never did see our friendly galloping Turtle again, and on the way back, as the Yacht bounced through the waters at speed, the neck strap of my brand-new Nikon F4 snapped seeing it fall into the ocean, never to be seen again. To this day the loss of that camera felt like a message from the Universe. *What you've seen here stays here. It was for your eyes only.*

The next and final stop was Melbourne and for me, the Universe had definitely saved the best for last.

When we arrived in Melbourne it was deemed safe enough for us to sight see and walk around the City alone. This was not the trivial decision it sounds; models are *insured* for vast amounts of money during work trips. (I was apparently insured for $2 Million when shooting for Coca-Cola in Italy). I remember stopping on Flinders Street Bridge and looking down at the murky rushing water of the Yarra River and imagining all kinds of murderous sea creatures hovering just beneath the ominous surface, it was after all an estuary and connected to the vastness of the ocean just a few city blocks away. I knew I'd never set foot in there, not in a million years, and as no-one else was either I pretty much gathered without being told to stay away from it. The wildness of the estuary rushed brazenly beneath the sophisticated city full of sculptures and artworks, galleries and museums, grand hotels and designer shops. The juxtaposition of the two was blinding. It was clear that people do manage to exist here and live a great life in the extreme heat and the sunshine, it's just that they do so by sharing the space with more killer spiders, snakes and jellyfish than any other nation on earth. It was as though Australians enjoyed living with the constant threat of death and their personalities seemed to carry an undercurrent of fuck-you-ness that I very much admired and still do today. I wouldn't say Australians are *Rough* around the edges more *Tough* around the edges and anyone coming here would be wise to remember that. This place takes no prisoners and though she now fights to take care of the poor and shelter the needy from other nations by allowing in refugees and immigrants, she is still the ruthless, harsh and unforgiving place I first came to in the early nineties. England may have sent her criminals here, and believe me, that thread is still apparent genetically in some, but the gene pool is also a cultural mix of Celts, Vikings, Italians and Greeks seeing their strong and immovable cultural personalities making for a rich society that is more diverse than anywhere else I have lived on earth. But what Australians had that I'd never seen anywhere else is *Heart* and despite being tough and brash they are never afraid to show their feelings. Grown men who can dead lift a washing machine will openly cry at *The Footie* their beloved Australian Rules football should they win, lose or the decision by the umpire not go their way. Australians watch 60 Minutes religiously as they hope to *Take Down the Bastards* when referring to crooks and wrong-doers caught out and they value their *old people* always seeming to understand that generations that went before them in this harsh place had a large hand in setting them up for their lives. I never had that here. I was what Aussies call a *First Generation Immigrant.* We do it tough, always having to gain traction without family help.

I told myself as I stood there on that bridge looking both down at the river and up at the mini-London that stood before me, close enough to be British, different enough not to be, that one day I would raise my children here, and I told myself I would move to Australia permanently by the year 2000. That was the age I told myself I would want children, thirty, thirty-one, and that instead of growing up in England as I had they would find their way here, among the spiders, and the snakes and the Australian people, who fascinated me so much. I wanted for them the freedom to speak, to work, to play in the sunshine and not be part of Europe. Though genetically I am what British people call a *Heinz 57 (a mix of many different cultural backgrounds)* being English, German and random gypsy genes believed to be Brazilian in origin or Romany *unclear because my Father was adopted* I have always felt very, very British. My home is full of items emblazoned with the Union Jack flag, my toaster, my fridge, my cups, my cushions and more, but last time I checked, which was around the time I left London forever in 2005, England didn't feel much like England anymore. It felt the way America is beginning to feel now. During the Wars invasions were more obvious, troops attempted to occupy, like the Nazi's in France, and everyone knew who the enemy was, but in our times the World is besieged by Trojan Horses. Some Nations who claim to come in peace offering gifts, harbor malevolent master plans to buy up everything and start making decisions, and crack it entirely when those plans get derailed. I am more than aware those

100

attempts go on in Australia, but in the UK and America they seemed to lose themselves beneath the weight of the invasions, unable to say no to the money being offered and happy to sacrifice what generations had fought to create and protect. Rather than be cultural melting pots they became cultural battlegrounds. I don't want my kids growing up around that and am constantly amazed that those causing racial and cultural tension are happy for their children to be raised within it. For example, I know that during the seven years I spent living in Los Angeles, and the prior annual modeling trips to Florida, I never saw racism personally in the USA, in fact racial diversity was everywhere. Yes, I may have been lucky, but I never felt America was a racist country or that Americans are inherently racist, so to see them accused of that now hurts. Luckily it hurts from afar. The closest I ever came to racism in Los Angeles was from *ME!* And it was totally accidental and not something I am proud of. I had just arrived in LA and was busy buying new towels at Bed, Bath & Beyond during a Sale, when my trolley came face to face with another in one of the very narrow isles. Without thinking, and in a very British voice I laughed and exclaimed,

It's a Mexican standoff!!!

Before realizing the person facing me, was actually Mexican. A rather uncomfortable moment I blame entirely on my childhood diet of American cartoons like Bugs Bunny and Foghorn Leghorn. Eek! How shitty I felt that day.

I wasn't quite sure *how* I was going to get back to Melbourne. I didn't have a master plan, so like everything else that happened in my life I left it to the wisdom and timing of the Universe. I decided to try and manifest it and so said out loud to the Yarra River Gods:

Help me find my way back please.

An indigenous artist who was selling his artwork on the bridge that day smiled at me, and I felt sure this meant that I would.

4

Flying into Barcelona was always like going home. I knew this place like the back of my hand and it was definitely another point on the graph. This time I was going to be able to spend some time with my model boyfriend who would also be shooting in Barcelona at the same time. In my mind he was always *on probation* in our relationship as I could tell that he often focused on the things he didn't like about me rather than the things he did and it left me feeling like I wasn't cherished. Something I learned much later on I very much need from a man. We were young, and he challenged me on all my beliefs, spiritually, politically and professionally but not in a healthy way, in a way to cause an argument, and I find arguments extremely tedious. He was a posh boy, from a wealthy family and had begun to feel more like an enemy than a partner and though I did feel love for him it was becoming more like a caring Sister than someone I wanted to be with sexually. Something was happening, something that reared its ugly head often in my relationships, and I never knew how to stop it. I will take full responsibility for being the cause however, and here is basically how it goes. I make a man feel powerful, successful and valued. This elevates his confidence, perhaps beyond what it should be, and he ends up believing the hype so strongly he begins undervaluing me, the very person who placed him high on that pedestal in the first place. The old-fashioned belief is that smart women, the ones who keep men for twenty or thirty years are those shrew and shrewd wives who sadly demolish their husband's self esteem and watch him hover in uncertainty for many, many years believing he can't do better. I cannot stand to see that, and it's happening everywhere. Those wives are more like jailers than life partners and monitor their spouses every move, even at work. Where he goes, who he speaks to, always making sure she injects enough poison and self doubt into his heart that he is too unsure of himself to hope for more from life. Though they may win the battle in the short term, those wives more often than not lose the War, with husbands either leaving after twenty years, unable to exist under the weight of the wife's control or simply undertaking endless affairs as a way to find shelter and refuge from her controlling nature, and perhaps exert some of their own, with a new and loving partner. If you are someone who thinks it's okay to treat your spouse this way, I would ask those of you who have children how you would feel about a partner that treated your child the way you treat your spouse? Most husbands say they feel like a walking ATM and in all honesty, they probably are. What's more disturbing than idle spouses who control and feel entitled to everything their hard-working partner worked for is that Courts often support them in the steal when they finally remove the mask and come after the assets of the poor sap who supported them for all those years. Laziness it seems is often rewarded in Court. *Oh but she sacrificed her career!* No, she simply chose not to work and was lucky enough not to have to.

So, despite his asking multiple times, I usually declined his offers of marriage despite his adorable Mother being very keen on the idea. I hope that somewhere deep inside he did love me, as we had been together for almost four years, but that Summer in Barcelona saw large helpings of doubt creep into my heart, and I knew we could never be. One of the models on this particular trip, an English girl was rather full of herself. She was *at her peak* as a female and was raking in perhaps half the amount of work I was, meaning she was making a very good living indeed, but for me it didn't matter who she was or how successful because she was not a good person inside. She was a gloater, a bragger and someone who displayed huge amounts of hubris. This she did at the pool one morning as I swam with my boyfriend. Her loud antics achieving her goal of gaining all the male attention within a sixty-foot radius, including my boyfriends, and when I rolled my eyes at the carry on, he said *She's just enjoying showing off her beautiful body.*

Argh the folly of youth, and in that moment he lost me. Not only was he defending her he was complimenting her at the same time. My relationship with him was over, whether he realized it or not, and I never slept with him again. You see loyalty and respect were and are a big thing for me. I have spent my life surrounded by male models and actors, all vying for my attention and have never made any of my partners feel threatened by that, I simply wouldn't. Even if I were not a model and simply that girl who worked in a Regional Bank Branch I wouldn't do it. So in a lesson I hope he learned that day, if not, he may be learning it now, I taught him the meaning of loyalty.

I didn't shed a single tear for any man I ended relationships with, not even those who fathered my children. Not because I was a cold Psychopath as their subsequent partners enjoyed labeling me, no, it was because I had labored long and hard over the decisions I made and was already out of love with them at the time I ended it. We live with standards that must be met all around us, competency at work, as citizens, as parents and as individuals and yet when standards fall well beyond what is acceptable within relationships, we seem to accept it. I had almost a compulsive need to *get away* from my partners when I knew we were finished, and luckily I always had the means to do it. Once I was emotionally gone I didn't even want them seeing me drink my morning coffee, it was that brutal.

So there I was, alone again in Barcelona, working and sight-seeing in one of my favorite cities in the World when I was contacted by my agent in London about a British catalogue shoot they were adding to my roster that month. She also asked me if I'd like to spend 2 weeks on a Yacht with her and her Billionaire Egyptian friend beforehand, and if so she would fly down in a few days time. I ummed and arghed, not having been the kind of girl who spends time on Billionaires Yachts, but as I had just become single and she was my trusted agent in London, I said yes, it couldn't hurt to have a better relationship with my her, and some girl-time sounded fun.

The Yacht was 79ft or 24 meters long and one of the grandest that was moored in the harbor. Two staff were milling around inside and always on board, a Chef and a Butler. As I stood on the jetty feeling the eyes of every tourist burning into me as they imagined the luxurious life I must be living I wondered how many Millions of his Billions of dollars this enormous and fantastically beautiful boat must have cost. I assumed it would be rather low rent to ask such a thing so decided against it. The waters around the Yacht seemed to somehow glisten more than the same water that lapped along the foreshore. This was because the water around the Yachts was much deeper and bluer than that at the beaches I was used to. Everything here was deep and lush, the waters, the Yacht *and* the attitudes. Our host appeared on the wooden walkway leading onto the boat in the Billionaires uniform of Armani suit worn casually over a T-shirt. He was about 25 years old, much younger than I had anticipated and introduced himself politely. He was clearly Arabic in some way and his golden skin and green eyes were easily good enough to see him lead a successful career as a male model, but I had the feeling this man had never had to work a day in his life. He was Egyptian, and the Egyptians I often met living in Europe tended to lead extremely privileged lives. It was 4pm in the afternoon and his Butler appeared at his side carrying a tray containing three glasses of Champagne. My London agent, who was a loud girl whooped with joy at the offering and yelped:

Whoohoo!!! Darllllings let's have some fun!

What followed was 14 days of Champagne fueled hedonism... by my booker. Not really a drinker in my early twenties and feeling uncomfortable in my strange surroundings I decided to be an observer and the person that would hold my friend up during the merriment. This was pretty much my pure personality coming through. I had never taken drugs at this point, never *zoned out* or got *plastered.* As you can tell I was a bundle of fun in my twenties, not. They say that Capricorns are born old and gradually grow younger. This is definitely true where I am concerned because at that time all I wanted was a simple life, so there was no need to become a mess in my down time it just wasn't for me. I guess this attitude must have been rare for a model holidaying on a rich Egyptians Yacht because he noticed me a little bit more than I'd expected. Or did he? As the days went on a small part of me began to believe that my booker from London had set up the whole event to marry me off to wealth. I dismissed it as another one of my conspiracy theories, and yet, there I was, single and unmarried on the Yacht of a single Billionaire Egyptian. I started to feel uneasy with the goings on, particularly when my female booker began getting *flirty* with me when drunk, and I told them I was feeling seasick and needed to go ashore. I had heard a phrase before sailing that boats get a foot shorter every day, and that had certainly been my experience of it. I couldn't wait to get off the Yacht, put my feet on dry land and be master of my own destiny once more instead of having to *check-in* to find out where we would be sailing next. I have never been comfortable being a passenger in life. For all the luxury it offered I only ever felt trapped and more like a captive than a guest. Our host was a complete gentleman the entire time and I respected him for that.

As requested, they took me ashore and onto the island where we travelled via limousine to his family home. High in the hills on the island of Majorca stood their imposing mansion protected by golden fencing and gates. It was as they say *too much,* grander than grand and more than a little intimidating. We walked through the huge double front doors and over the ivory marble flooring to the vast pool area where a petite woman, beautifully dressed was kneeling facing the ocean. She was praying and our host advised we didn't disturb her. He showed me to my room and I decided to take a shower. Inside the showerhead, taps and drain were also golden like the fencing and gates. My small hand struggled to turn the enormous taps as four giant jets, that I later discovered were *solid gold,* supplied what was quite simply the best shower I've ever had. Feeling as though I had been exfoliated by the powerful water and dressing for the evening, I emerged again to the pool area where the elegant and petite lady was now seated reading French Vogue. She stood to face me and I could feel every fiber of her assessing me. I knew exactly what for, I'm not an idiot, and I realized that coming ashore had if anything made matters worse. Suddenly my booker arrived behind me loudly and began an oral resume of my work and achievements to the somewhat bemused woman, who I now assumed was our hosts Mother. I was right, he emerged and introduced us all and they spoke privately for just a moment. Her face and body language seemed to be suggesting that my booker wasn't welcome, and I was pretty sure my booker had caught the gist of it too. The lady nodded her head at me and only me and slowly walked inside. He spoke.

My Mother won't be joining us for dinner. She isn't feeling well.

Argh, the Universal *get-out-of-jail-free* card for parents. Note to self: always use that one.

We swam in the pool, ate Lobsters, sunbathed and shopped in the town for the remaining two days of our trip before the last evening arrived ahead of our flights, hers back to London and mine to Barcelona. I watched the sunset from the terrace alone, contemplating being single for the first time in many years, my booker not emerging as she usually did, when I felt our host appearing at my side silently. His English was impeccable having been educated in London and I realized before he spoke that the entire trip had been a fourteen-day audition process and I was reasonably sure what was going to happen next.

He proposed, not on one knee, but took my hand gently in a manner that said *I will always treat you kindly* and spoke.

I wanted to ask you if you would do me the honor of accepting my proposal of marriage?

I had never in my life been the kind of girl who wanted, expected or had even fantasized about being proposed to, and my English boyfriends proposals were never romantic, but it was however shockingly beautiful and complimentary as this handsome Egyptian whispered the words to me. He stood before me with bright green hopeful eyes in his Armani suit next to an azure blue pool with golden pool ladder, and I realized what was missing from this scenario. Love.
I spoke respectfully and honestly from my heart.

I am extremely flattered that a man as lovely as you would ask me that, but I cannot marry you. I don't love you and you deserve someone who does.

He seemed to have expected a knock back and took it well adding:

I wanted to take care of you, for you to be "alright" for the rest of your life, be safe and taken care of.

No-one had ever said that to me before. The strength of it was so moving that I almost changed my mind, but my first words had been the wisest and I rubbed the top of his hand to show him that I really did want the best for both of us.

He asked me if we could be lifelong friends, to which I said yes, knowing that when I flew away from that place the following day, I would never see him or speak with him again. I heard that he asked three other models from Elite for their hand in marriage that year, and I hoped that instead of finding someone *he could take care of* he'd be lucky enough to find someone who wanted to take care of *him.*

My booker didn't speak to me for a month, and following the trip our relationship was never the same, I could feel her disappoint in me after she heard about how I declined his hand in marriage and I got the feeling she considered me a *lost cause* for needing to find true love. Later that year she would introduce me to a fifteen-year-old model who was dating *(illegally)* an aging rock star and the introduction was meant as a *This is what smart girls do* moment. The rock star in question was gross as well as a paedophile in my opinion, and I remained very happy about who I was and the decisions I was making.

I spent the next two to three years working solidly despite the crippling negativity coming from my agent who would tell me that I was too old at *22,23,24, too fat* and *too short* almost consistently each time I dropped in. She would often remind me,

It's fingers down the throat time for you missy.

I never did throw up anything I'd eaten. I must have been such a disappointment to her. It didn't wear me down, I was already too damaged by life for their words to hurt me, and though they didn't know it, telling me I couldn't do something, was like a red rag to a bull. I began a cycle of not caring what happened to me, some call it bravery, but I was prepared to go anywhere, try anything and make sure that I was as far away from a Regional Bank Branch as I could possibly get. I didn't want to rely on a man. There had certainly been no men in my life that had shown themselves to be dependable, and so I became a lone Wolf, traveling, working and silently leading a very lonely life, a life I had chosen to live.

A few weeks later I had decided to make a conscious effort to meet *nice guys,* and possibly someone who would be more my type. Friends of mine had invited me to a private dinner party in Mayfair to make up a foursome on a blind date with a Plastic Surgeon. The dinner was a lot of fun and though I learned some interesting tips about anti-aging I certainly couldn't see myself dating him, but as the dinner had gone well, we decided to repeat the gathering at the Dorchester Hotel a week later. I had never stayed at the Dorchester Hotel before or eaten dinner there and was very impressed with the lavish cheese and dessert trolleys that were brought to the table. It was almost too grand for words for a girl in her early twenties from Worcestershire, and I remember feeling a little dizzy in the surroundings. I excused myself to the bathroom where I took a moment to face myself in the mirror and question what the hell I was doing there. These weren't my kind of people; this wasn't my kind of place and I raced out of there ready to say my goodbyes and head home. As I did I smacked headlong into a handsome boy who seemed very familiar.

Jesus Christ I'm so sorry!

Said the boy with a strong American accent.
He had blue eyes and fair hair and I could smell marijuana on his breath as he hung there for a couple of seconds too long following his apology.

Are you, are you, here with somebody?
He asked nervously.

I was, but I'm leaving. I have a big drive home.

I replied.

We stood there the two of us, contemplating the next move, he licking his lips furiously, very much his trademark, and I motioning backwards towards the dining room when he asked,

Would you have dinner with here tomorrow night? I mean, not here, not in the restaurant, in my room? I'm staying here and well, it would be nice to know somebody, anybody in this town, by way of an apology?

He looked sweet, and kind, and I knew how it felt to be in a hotel room a long way from home and not know anybody, and so I said,

Yes.

I spent the next couple of months as his lover at the Dorchester hotel. Turns out he was a Hollywood actor filming in London for just a short time. He mostly smoked pot and ate junk food as we watched movies and relaxed during his down time. He was one of the good guys I felt, someone I should be able to love, but I just didn't, and so when he asked me to return to Los Angeles with him after filming, I declined. I never did have any big plans to move to LA, my dream was Australia, and so the boy who spoke nervously and licked his lips a lot and I, said goodbye, as my hunt for Love rolled on. If you think it's odd that I am not *naming* Lovers in an attempt to draw publicity, I can assure you it is not. Many well-known people share intimate relationships with other celebs and no-one ever hears about them. It keeps a small part of a very public life private and without this unspoken integrity most celebs would never have sex at all!

Despite being a young model living in London I had never stepped foot in a London Nightclub. My agency was holding their annual *New Faces* competition, where literal teenagers could win the chance to become *the next big thing* and my disgruntled agent insisted I come along as one of their girls. The invitation was very last minute and I had a suspicion that perhaps a few people had pulled out. She also made it very clear that I owed her one for declining the Billionaire so I agreed to go along. I wore an outfit that I felt would allow me to dance which consisted of vintage white patent leather knee high zip up boots *very 60's* a bright yellow mini-skirt that I had bought in Miami not knowing when I would wear it, and a bikini top in black and red, I was after all a swimwear model. I have been photographed many times in the little yellow mini-skirt and when I see the photographs it always makes me smile.

My tan was always deep and rich from chasing Summer around the globe for photo shoots and I know that my agents were more than a little surprised by my outfit when they saw me arrive. Their attitude towards me changed drastically that night and they started dragging me this way and that to meet famous people, and I had a sneaking feeling they were *at it again*, as at the back of the club, which seemed vast, was a private VIP section, roped off with a giant red rope sporting gold hooks at either end that looked like it had been lifted from the Titanic. I wasn't really a film buff and so though faces were familiar I couldn't place them. The only movies I had seen at the cinema at that point were Flash Gordon, ET and Star Wars. I was however very into music, not the techno stuff that was emerging in the nineties but bands like The Sisters of Mercy. An older man who I later learned was a

manager type hauled me over and introduced me to Tom
Cruise. I beamed a smile as broad as any Julie Roberts could
give, not because he was Tom Cruise but because he really did
look like Paul from Walkabout Creek. He took one look at me,
as if I had been offered up as a sacrifice and shook his head at
the manager, and just like that I had been rejected by the real
Tom Cruise without ever really knowing what I was being
offered for. Next, a small man with very long eyelashes was
introduced who I later learned was the singer/ songwriter
Prince. I thought at first he might be gay but as the evening
progressed it was apparent he was not, as he slowly became
surrounded by beautiful young girls. It was sweaty and
overcrowded in the VIP section, and from where I was
standing it was far more *uncomfortable* behind the velvet rope
than in front of it and so I headed out to get some fresher air.
But as I got to the Titanic rope a huge bouncer literally picked
me up off the floor leaving my feet dangling beneath me and
carried me back deep into the VIP section. I wriggled like a
child being chastised by a parent and demanded he put me
down, panicking about the reliability of my bikini top, as his
giant fingers squeezed into my arms with a force that would
surely be leaving bruises. My heart began to race as I could

have no defense against such a brute and he placed me on the knee of a very muscular man, a man whose face I knew from childhood.

Are you Rocky? I asked.

I am yes! And you are? Said a very jovial Sylvester Stallone.

I'm nobody, absolutely nobody. I clarified.

You don't want to be sitting here do you? Said the man mountain.

No I don't. I replied sheepishly feeling very much like a child.

To which he instructed his bodyguard to *take care* of whatever *needs* I might have for the night and he smiled a kind goodbye.

People used to say to me that *Girls like you don't say no to guys like that.* Thing is, I genuinely didn't know at the time what I was saying no to, that's how naïve I was. But I am damned grateful that I did decline the unknown with a whole assortment of *eligible men* that I seemed to be placed before as a model. I don't want to meet someone in that way, like Sushi they might consider ordering. I didn't want any one-night-stands with celebrities who saw me as a piece of meat. I wanted to fall in love, be knocked off my feet, feel like I'm dying when they kiss me and have them care about what's best for me *outside* as well as *inside* the bedroom. Bumping into the Hollywood actor outside a bathroom was fine, but being *chosen* in a nightclub full of models, was definitely not. Was I expecting too much waiting for Love? Life would teach me that yes, it probably was too much to expect.

5

It was a rare warm night in London, probably why the club felt so stuffy and so eventually I felt a need to get outside. The next teenage hottie had been crowned and subsequently introduced to the assembled male celebs and so I felt ducking outside wouldn't be a crime, not like the crimes I felt were being committed inside the club, as under aged females were offered up to wealthy and famous older men for light conversation in a nightclub. I'd had a cheeky glass of Champagne or two just to cope and it had made me strangely weepy as I wasn't used to drinking, so I found a clean-ish looking stone step opposite the club in the tiny mews, and sat down for a lonely, girlie cry at the state of the World. I felt my face getting hot as the salty tears rolled down, simultaneously ruining my make-up and drying out my skin at the same time, but by then I couldn't have given a fuck, I was having a conservative moment, and no-one was going to take it away from me. I was 22 years old and a full 9 years older than the *New Face* that had just been crowned. I was beginning to understand why my agent thought I was too old to be a

London model, why she was desperately trying to marry me of to wealth and I didn't like the feeling at all. I wasn't just too *old* to be a model, I was too mature and too damn smart to put up with the unsavory characters it placed me around. I was 22 for crying out loud! No-one should feel old at 22! I leaned forward onto my knees and took some deep breathes, unsure I was going to be able to go back inside, when some large feet appeared in tan shoes in front of me. On top of the tan shoes were some worn-in looking green jeans and on top of that a vest top barely covering a very muscular and tanned torso. It had taken me a while to get to the vest as the legs belonged to a 6ft 2in Australian male. I blinked and tried to clear my eyes before eventually seeing a blonde man with long hair and blue eyes staring down at me. He couldn't have looked *more* Australian if he'd tried, barely beaten to the punch by Crocodile Dundee's Paul Hogan.

You alright slim? You look like you're having a shocker?

He laughed, betraying one of the broadest Aussie accents I had ever heard.

With smudged make-up and blurry unglamorous eyes, I squinted up at him, which hurt my neck as he was an amazon. He certainly wasn't frightening in any way as he stood above me on the cobbles of the rainy London mews, but at the same time I had no idea who he was. His mate was also a literal man mountain.

Turns out he was another celeb there that night, but like me had also had enough of the goings on inside. He invited me to an underground club in Old Street, the cool part of town at the time, and I declined, sighting a need to *stay with my friends.* Having never been out to club in London ever before, I felt two outings in one night might be a bit daring. However, the tall Australian insisted my friends were invited too and that he had a big car, and eventually, after much consternation, I went inside to invite them. When they clapped eyes on the tall Australian whose name I still didn't know one pulled me aside and said,

OMG it's Brad you have to shag him and then tell us what it was like!

What followed was two years of a very comfortable boyfriend-girlfriend relationship, well I thought so anyway. I certainly never felt a desire for marriage or anything permanent and so when in 1995 he asked me if I wanted to move back to Melbourne, Australia with him it came as something of a surprise. But the clever Universe had timed the whole event perfectly. He had been offered an acting role back home, and I needed to move territory again, as I had become *overexposed.* My face was everywhere in the UK and people were basically sick of seeing me.

And then it hit me, I had asked for this. Even though I had spent two years living with this Australian in London it had never occurred to me that he might one day want to go *home.* He was the veritable King of London society and I felt he was in the UK for good, nothing like the American boy who was just visiting. I had left the timing and decision to the Gods, and they had worked their magic very cleverly. Should I give it a go down under with this Australian? Of course, so I sold my BMW car to the DJ Brandon Block, who complained later that the engine had fallen off its mounts one night as he drove to the North of England, and packed up my life. Oh, how I miss the days when everything I owned could be packed into four suitcases. I gave my homely bits to family and took the twenty-eight-hour flight back down under.

This time however would be different, this time I had an Australian boyfriend but was completely on my own professionally. There would be no clients, no chauffeurs, no schedules, no jobs, just me and my own survival skills to get me through.

As he had to travel ahead of me to do clothing fittings for his role, I decided to stop off in Bali *alone* for 12 days to decompress before diving headlong into my new life. I regretted it almost as soon as I arrived, as Bali was full of surfers and hippie types that weren't really my scene and I felt instantly homesick for the UK, which hardly ever happened. I lay on the sundrenched beaches alone and told myself that I must have needed this space for *some* reason, and set about trying to work out why. Day two put paid to any plans I had for self examination on the island when, suffering from jetlag and approaching Christmas after another long, hard year of work I fell asleep on my back on a beach towel for six hours. How I wasn't robbed blind of my phone, room key and wallet as I lay there I'll never know but shortly after waking and feeling relief about that I felt the terrifying pain of sunburn from head to toe but particularly on my face, and it was agony. I ran to the resort pharmacy and bought up bottles of Calamine Lotion and Aloe Vera and retired to my beach hut to assess the damage. My face was tomato red, as if I had flown too close to the sun or been mildly fried next to some bacon and eggs. I soaked my face and body with everything I could get my hands on, moisturizer, aloe and lotion, until eventually I fell asleep again and woke in horror to find the skin on my cheeks was hard, like fried bacon and with my nails I could tap it and hear a clicking sound. My forehead was a mass of dry wrinkles and my nose felt like it may suddenly fall off. I told myself I had blown it; my modeling career was surely over now and without plastic surgery the *burning* would leave me forever changed. I lay in a darkened room for days. Then, three days later, as the pink/red burn began to turn a deep red/ brown I felt an itching sensation as I woke on my nose. I gently tapped the side with my nail and the skin *moved.* It was like something from a horror film, when a large figure of eight shape left to right on both cheeks and across my nose simply *SLID OFF.* The next day the skin on my forehead did the same. I looked in the mirror and realized how much I had taken for granted, the reason why I had been a successful model for years, the pure *chance* of looking a certain way, and now I had blown it. The skin underneath the peel looked more pink, fragile and juicy than anything I had ever seen and along the edges where the peel ended and the old skin remained were large and very obvious *tea stains.* I suddenly didn't look like a model anymore. I didn't even look like Nicola Charles. I looked like some typical English idiot who had burned on day one of a holiday. The whole thing was madness, I was a seasoned traveller, a seasoned sunbather and it was my first taste of how *the Sun* in the Southern hemisphere is a very different animal. Just like the sun loungers in Alice Springs I had been stripped of my veneer, and I had absolutely no idea how my Australian boyfriend or my agent were going to feel about it. Luckily he was on hand with advice from a prominent plastic surgeon friend who told me:

You have essentially given yourself a chemical peel. Your skin will recover, I will give you something to help remove the tea stain edging, but then, you must NEVER allow this new skin to burn again.

130

I learned a valuable lesson on that trip about life down under, one that Aussie kids are now routinely taught in school. Under no circumstances can you mess with the Australian Sun *EVER,* because it doesn't matter what your heritage or background is, or how well your skin coped in the rest of the World, the Aussie Sun will get you, and it will win.

My Australian and I were getting lots of attention from photographers, with my deep tan also being something of a talking point in the press, causing much discussion about my *heritage,* and within weeks a cover appeared on a street newspaper called *The Truth* with the headline *British Supermodel Lands in Melbourne.* It was quite a flattering thing at the time as I was getting too old to model in London and was certainly not a Supermodel. I remember my boyfriend's sister looking at the cover and commenting,

So typical of Melbourne, a new head arrives in town and they lose their shit over it!

Having featured in long-running, highly successful TV ad campaigns in the UK, dealing with my boyfriend's TV stardom and the attention we got as a couple felt like a doddle. In the nineties Melbourne felt about half as populated as it does today and life was easy and fun. Press photographers snapping us tipsy and leaving nightclubs didn't bother me too much at all and so for the most part life bowled along pretty much as I would have wanted it to. Then the phone rang and it was my agent back in the UK, I had been offered a beauty campaign for a well-known brand of shampoo and conditioner, one girl was going to be shampoo and the other Conditioner *(Me)*. The paycheck was vast and required a two-day shoot back in London the following week. I had no choice I had to accept the booking. So, off I travelled back to London to work, with the plan to head straight back to Australia afterwards. One of the requirements for the job was that my hair be as dark as possible without being black for *the look* the client wanted. I had always had naturally light brown hair with golden highlights that flooded in from the Sun, and I felt sad that the beauty of it was going to be gone, but for 90,000 UK pounds I found the compromise doable. For three solid days back in London I was sent to a ritzy W1 Tricologist. They were nothing to do with the famous shampoo brand, but had been instructed to make my hair both darker and shine like never before to accommodate the rear slow motion shot of me dropping my impossibly shiny hair down my tanned back. I spent three days having *real* Avocado's, Cucumbers and other fruits mushed unceremoniously into my very long hair. The hair was then wrapped in cloth while I sat under a mild heat lamp for hours munching on carrots and green tea. At the time I thought the whole exercise was pointless and tedious, until on day three the result was revealed, and blow me down with a feather if I didn't have the shiniest hair you had ever seen. I will never forget the conversation I had with an art director the day we shot the ad campaign.

Can I take some of the product home? My Mum really likes it. I asked.

And with a look of abject horror he pulled me gently aside and said,

God no whatever you do don't use the product. Ever! It's literally Fairy Liquid re-packaged!

I shot the ad, decided against taking the product and took myself and my newly darkened hair back to Oz.

Within about two weeks of being back in Melbourne I was feeling restless. My Australian had headed up to Queensland in my absence to film and I was now holidaying in his home *alone*. I joined Chadwick models the following week and immediately started shooting. One of the strangest things about Australia in the nineties was that the popular television shows seemed to be about twenty-years behind the UK with all age demographics watching shows like *The Price is Right*. I watched on with amusement as they would yell the answers at the screen and become totally involved in a show that had been axed in the UK in the eighties for having a dated format (*though it returned again years later*). The girls on the show were *models* but seemed to be more what Britons describe as *Promotions Girls,* being part model, part sales rep. I found their formulaic and unnatural speaking techniques when talking about washing machines, cars and holidays, whilst posing in a bikini sporting maniacal grins truly bizarre, and I jokingly said to my boyfriend's sister:

What an incredibly easy way to make a living! No Art directors! No re-takes! No travelling! Just day after day at the same studio in a bikini showing off prizes.

And so the next day, as I realized that modeling work in Melbourne, Australia might not keep me as busy as I was used to in London, I decided to pay the lovely people at *The Price is Right* a little visit from a British girl.

My boyfriend's sister had lent me her old Datsun car to use until I bought my own. It was no Renault, or Land Rover or BMW but it got me from A to B in the small city of Melbourne, and as long as I kept the biscuit wheels out of the tram tracks, she didn't wobble around too much. It was summer, and with the downside of no working air-conditioning it meant I had to drive her with at least the drivers window down, meaning bad hair days and the possibility of swallowing a large Australian flying insect. I tried to see the humor in it but on this particular day I decided I'd try and sweat it out and keep the windows up, so as to have *Price is Right* perfect hair.

As I approached a crossroads with traffic lights the large
Range Rover Vogue HSE in front of me ducked into another
lane, to avoid the tram tracks, meaning the old Datsun and I
had to wobble onto the tracks to remain in lane at the junction
and get through the next green light. A car in front of the
Range Rover who was going left had to wait to turn for a
pedestrian crossing the road meaning woweeee! I got ahead of
the fancy Range Rover when the lights turned green. *This*
seemingly enraged the *Witch of Toorak* driving the beast who,
not wishing to be outdriven, proceeded to closely tailgate me
for a number of kilometers in a desperate attempt to find an
opportunity to return the favor. Eventually the large car
appeared next to my driver's window as the blonde lady with
lips the size of a Baboons bottom motioned for me to wind my
window down. I thought she might be about to tell me that the
Datsun had a brake light out or that I had failed to observe
some unseen Australian traffic law on my journey. Instead,
after I attempted to open the window with dignity, only to see
it drop like a stone into the door crack, she hollered from her
pedestal:

WHY DON'T YOU GO BACK TO WHERE YOU CAME FROM YOU FILTHY FUCKING WOG!

A little bit bemused I replied,

Erm filthy? sorry what did you say? I'm British?

And with that she sped off as if she were the pace car in the Australian Grand Prix. Cars honked their horns behind me as I sat there somehow knowing I had been dealt some kind of racial slur and attack, but unsure of the lingo I eventually pulled away desperately trying to close the manual window through which the verbal diatribe had been slung but to no avail. I was now feeling *"less than"*, *bullied* and *looking a bit windswept*, but determined to learn what manner of insult I had been dealt later on from the wisdom of my boyfriends Sister. I tried to gather myself from the road rage incident for my meeting with *The Price is Right*, which incidentally I didn't have. That's right, I was going to attempt a *Walk-in*, my personal specialty, always a fan of the element of surprise, and like a true pro I gathered my shit *into one sock*, as Aussies like to say, and marched windswept, insulted and determined into the offices of Grundy Television in South Melbourne. Who was I there to see? Dunno. Did I have any idea how to attempt the initial contact? No. Did I continue regardless? Abso-fucking-lutely.

You see my outlook on life is this, our time here is short, do you want to spend it procrastinating or do you want to actually achieve some of the things you want to do? If you do, then stop waiting for life to come to you and go out and find what you are looking for. As I often say, life has no remote, you have to get up and change it.

(FYI imho this rule does not work for Love, no, no, no. Love, must come and find you, and will usually do so when you least expect it).

The vast reception area at Grundy Television was predictably white and minimalist, and a pretty receptionist sat almost obscured by an unusually high reception desk that made sure only her pretty little head was visible. I took out my heavy book *(model portfolio)* from my bag and explained that I had just arrived in Australia from London and was here to leave my details for *The Price is Right.* To her credit she realized a model from London was something worth entertaining and took my book. She had only seen the first two pages before saying decisively:

Take a seat.

Feeling pleased with the outcome I settled down for whatever kind of wait was coming, models are used to waiting, sometimes for hours, particularly those of us who rocked up unannounced. At the far end of the reception area was an elevator and within about five minutes there was a loud *ping* signifying the doors were about to open. I expected a junior member of show casting to pop out but instead an older lady with piercing blue eyes and short grey hair bounced out confidently and spoke with another very strong Australian accent.

Nicola? Hello darling I'm Jan Russ, come with me. How very lovely of you to come down and see us.

Her greeting was odd, as if she had been expecting me, as she seemed to know who I was. I couldn't have known at the time, but nothing went on in Melbourne without Jan knowing about it, not when it came to casting. On an upper level she walked me into a largish room that contained a blue screen at one end with a single chair placed in front of it. It was pretty run of the mill for television and wearing my best bikini underneath my clothing I assumed that like most castings for a job that involved wearing swimsuits I would need to be seen in mine. Placed casually on the chair were some script pages and I picked them up before sitting down. The lady then put her glasses on the end of her nose and said:

First we'll do your name and agent details and then we'll read okay?

I nodded and glanced down for the first time at the pages, expecting to see the show title *The Price is Right* at the top of the page. Instead in bold black and strangely familiar lettering was the word ***Neighbours.*** I quickly sifted through the five or six pages to see if it had become mixed up somehow with pages from *The Price Is Right*. Nope, they were all Neighbours script pages.

Erm, I think I may be in the wrong room. I said.

Don't think so darling. She replied.

Yes. No. I mean I'm here for The Price is Right. This is my book. I'm a model.
And I motioned my portfolio in her direction.

Leaning forward in her chair she pushed her glasses to the tip of her nose and glared over the top with those piercing blue eyes to say,

I'm sure it's very nice and I can see what you have here.

She said, drawing an invisible line around her face.

But what I want to know is what is going on inside, and she pointed to her temple.

I don't know if any of you have ever been in a situation where you've attended an interview for a job, only to be ushered in for a different one that far exceeded any expectations you had for yourself, but I can tell you now the few seconds I had to adjust were not enough.

I glanced down at the pages again realizing that I had two choices, I could cut and run or I could say the damn lines, get out of there, and tell myself this never happened. I decided to go with the latter. Sure, I'd *acted* in approximately sixty Worldwide television commercials but creating a long running character that people could believe and relate to was a whole different ball game. Oh yes, and I had about 10 seconds to *Create* the persona of **Sarah**. She wasn't on the page, instead I was reading a character that was on the show called Dani, but I knew that whatever Jan Russ was hoping to see and find in me that day needed to be unique and memorable. In the ten seconds I had to prepare I thought of the all the less favorable personality traits my Mother had teased me about and the most overriding one was *Moodiness.* So I read the as yet non-existent character, speaking the words of a real character already on the show, via a model who didn't expect to be doing this that day and with ten seconds to prepare.

After the first read she stopped and placed her pages gently in her lap before removing her glasses to address me.

Well, well, well, who's this then? I liked that Nicola. I liked it a lot. Let's read that again.

To this day I cannot tell you what the words on that page were. They filtered into me as the borrowed and unexpected narrative they were and on the way through scraped up some of my most overriding personality traits and dragged them from my lips and into reality. Hearing myself *BE* someone else was almost as exciting as an orgasm. It was as if someone had given me a drug, as surely massive amounts of dopamine flooded into my brain, giving me a combination of *buzz* and *mischievous confidence.* It was clear for Jan to see that despite the abrupt and unexpected nature of the *Audition* I had managed to run with it. She paused, legs crossed, pages on her lap, holding her glasses like a pen she was about to write with.

I want to go and get some more scripts if that's alright. I won't be long.

And with that she disappeared from the room. So many questions filled my mind as I sat there feeling very much like a cast member in a David Lynch movie.

How had this happened? Who was that who just came through me like a medium? Was that the real me? A different side of me perhaps? Had I just created an impromptu character?

After returning with more pages and different characters lines, which I delivered as *my invented character of Sarah (though the name was not in existence at that time)* she eventually stood, walked over and shook my hand. Something interesting had happened in that room that day, but only one of us had the power to do anything about it. Shell shocked and inexperienced I nervously thanked her, feeling strangely embarrassed, as if she had seen me naked, which of course in a sense she had, because acting is being naked, and hightailed it out of there, vowing to never tell another soul about what just happened. For her part Jan Russ was nothing like other Casting Directors I had met for commercials. She herself had something very special, an eye, an attitude, experience, I've never successfully put my finger on it, but she had an ability to find parts of a person they didn't know were there, and bring them to the surface, and for that, I will be eternally grateful. Like a wild and immature pony, she broke me in that day and I grew up. I had been pushed to find another level, another layer of myself, a layer deep down inside I hadn't shared with many, and had encouraged me to coax it out.

I don't remember the drive home in the rusty old red Datsun in the heat. I don't remember anything about the following two days after the audition. I shut down, still in shock, and simply behaved mechanically, brushing teeth, drinking coffee, running and wondering if she might *tell anybody* that she managed to strip a layer off a British model that turned up one day. I told my agent about the *Price Is Right* mix up but no-one else. The feeling very much reminded me of heartache after a breakup. Like that strange feeling of embarrassment that someone who had known you so intimately was no longer in your life. Then on day two, and I am livid that I can't remember the *exact* date, as it is probably one of the most important of my entire life, the phone rang while I was carrying a giant Pizza box into my boyfriend's sister who was sick in bed. It was my agent from Chadwick Models in Melbourne.

Hi Nicola you clever girl, are you sitting down? My agent said.

Nope, I am carrying a Pizza. I replied.

Then put it somewhere and sit down luvvy. Your life is about to change.

I placed the pizza box on the bed and went into the kitchen to sit. I genuinely imagined I had landed another clothing campaign in Australia having recently shot for Bullet Jeans.

*We've had a call from Jan Russ at **Neighbours.** She wants you to do a screen test for a permanent role on the show. If it goes well, they will write you in.*

It was a lot to take in. I remained silent while I tried to process what she was saying.

Hello Nicola did you hear me? There was no audition, right? You just turned up? Your Price Is Right mix up? Well done for doing that, because now they are going to write a character and storyline around you. Which is phenomenal. Say something?

Right. Wow. I really didn't think I'd ever hear from her again. I replied.

The pages are being couriered to you tomorrow and your screen test is on Tuesday next week. Prepare for it, this will be the most important audition of your life.

I walked into the bedroom of my boyfriend's sister who was ill in bed holding a large floppy slice of Hawaiian Pizza.

What the hell has happened? She asked.

I'm screen testing for a role on Neighbours next week.

She screamed with delight. You see that was the show that had made her Brother famous, and suddenly, and randomly, after

an attempt to be a model on *The Price is Right,* I was heading
in that direction too. Possibly, probably, depending on the
screen test, the all-important screen test.

It was the day of filming.

I was taken from reception through the Production offices,
bustling with writers, producers and assistants, past the
greenrooms, which smelled musty and very much like
someone needed to open a window, and out onto the back lot.
Outside was a set I vaguely recognized from British television,
but it wasn't from *Neighbours* it was the Prison from *Prisoner
Cellblock H.* Just the sight of the huge brick walls without
windows brought that very unique theme tune flooding back
into my head. The one I used to fall asleep listening to because
my Mother was downstairs watching it as I slowly drifted off
in bed.

I had never watched *Neighbours* growing up, but at college
was aware that its lunchtime airing was very popular in the
common room with the other students. It felt odd being around
the real life set of something that had almost become a
religion in the UK, and I reminded myself to respect that.

The *set* for my screen test comprised of a small metal table
and two chairs outside the Café, which wasn't really a café,
just a giant piece of painted wood with what looked like
railway girders holding it up at the back. The light at that time
of day was dim but, on the table and chairs it was bright
sunshine, thanks to the wizardry of the lighting guys who had
flooded the scene in a golden warmth that screamed
Australian Soap Opera!

Then, a petite blonde arrived from between the cameramen
wearing a dressing gown, sloppy boots and biting into an
apple. She looked tired, the kind of girl who had been up all-
night partying before being dragged into work and fixed up by
hair and make-up. I'd met those girls before as a model but
this one also had a massive odor of *Bitch* radiating all around
her. She plonked herself unceremoniously down on the chair
and put her booted feet up on the table as she eyed me
suspiciously. Jan Russ approached and handed us both scripts.

Sorry, I didn't get chance to look at it. The actress said
insincerely. *Busy day.*

Jan re-assured her it was okay for her to read as only I would
be on camera and we prepared to start.
Still crunching into her apple, she told me without words that
she was in *no way* going to make it easy for me.
They called *Action* and I began speaking.

She jumped in suddenly, *Wait, wait, wait, oooohhhhh we're
doing that bit? Okay my bad, sorry let's start again.*

I began the dialogue again, and as I finished my line,
expecting hers to follow she gave me nothing. Dead air. I
didn't know what to do, the cameras were rolling, she was
being a total bitch and had now made it clear that de-railing
my screen test was her number one mission, so again, just like
at Grundy television, I rallied.

I decided to continue with my share of the lines and fuck hers,
roll them into one dialogue, all the while looking intensely
into her eyes, daring her to chime in, her involvement being
the only thing that would stop me speaking.

150

The freedom it gave me to arbitrarily cut her lines was exhilarating, and for just a moment I saw a faint glimmer of respect in her eyes. She lowered the apple for the first time and leant forward, acting her arse off despite not being on camera, and joined in. What followed was two minutes of what can only be described as a snide, mean spirited, spiteful diatribe that when finished saw a cameraman clear his throat from the shock of it. Without leaving my gaze for a second, making sure her threatening behavior landed exactly where she wanted it to, she said,

Are we done?

Yes. Yes, you are. Said Jan Russ.

Jan followed the actress as she left the set and headed back to the studios and though I couldn't hear what she was saying, the body language did not look good.

My agent said nothing about the screen test for two weeks, and I got on with the business of living, and flew to Queensland to see my boyfriend. While up there I was asked to do a photo shoot for a charity with their Ambassador the British motorbike racer Barry Sheene. It was a spur of the moment request and excited to again meet the man who used to race against my Dad I proceeded to have a long and very frank talk with him about how much better Australia is than the UK. For Sheene even more so, as he went into detail about just how many pins and wires were now holding his damaged body together, and how he was unable to remain in the UK because the pins created pain in a damp environment. The trip was a great distraction from worrying about the screen test and I made sure not to tell *anyone* about it, not even my family back in the UK.

Upon my return the phone once again rang and the words said were truly surprising.

Hi Nicola, so congrats! You've been offered a two-year contract with Neighbours as a series regular. You have a six months probation period, during which time they will assess if it's going well or not, and then you're home free. The character is called Jane Beaumont and she is a British model who has recently re-located to Melbourne. Shouldn't be too hard that one should it? She quipped. *We can't negotiate your contract past what they've offered, which is standard, but after the initial two-years you'll have a lot of power at re-negotiation phase. We are so, so proud of you! Wow! We send girls down there all the time and they never get a sniff, so right time, right place for you my girl.*

It was late, and I looked out of the massive windows into the night. In just over two weeks I had gone from being a model to an actor thanks to my efforts to get on *The Price is Right*. I felt proud, nervous, excited, fearful all at the same time, but one thing I was absolutely sure about was that *no way on God's earth* was my character name being *Jane*. It was the name of a bully I disliked at school and I'd be damned if I was going to make it famous!

6

I had gone through the entire process of trying to get on *The
Price is Right* with my newly darkened hair, dyed by the client
for the British Shampoo commercial, but I didn't like it. It felt
harsh and gothic and I very much wanted it returned to
somewhere near normal before I started filming. One of the
things I had insisted on in my *Neighbours* contract was that I
do my own hair and make-up. It was something I was advised
to do by my boyfriend, who having worked on the show
before recommended it. Not because the hair & make-up
artists on the show weren't any good, but because as someone
who was already a Brand, known as Nicola Charles the model,
I had to protect it. However, within that was a clause that
stated I must first check with the show before changing hair
colour or length. The reply came swiftly and directly, *there
was to be absolutely no change to my hair colour as Jane
Beaumont was going to be a bad guy.*

I was stuck with the damned dark hair! Why are girls with
dark hair the bad guys? Oh I suppose blondes are all
sweetness and light are they? The face of the blonde with

Baboons lips calling me a *Filthy fucking Wog!* from her Range Rover flashed before my eyes, along with literally every other hateful blonde I had ever known. I wasn't aware of being *the bad guy* in any TV commercials I'd done when I had light brown hair?

Oh yes, and I urgently needed to change that character name!

Luckily the writers were happy to do that, and by the time my first scripts arrived the characters name had been changed at my request to the name of a girl I had quite liked at school...

Sarah Beaumont

She was here. She had been born.

Right there on the page.

It was immediately obvious from the initial character breakdown and subsequent dialogue that Ms. Beaumont was going to be quite an interesting girl to play. She was deceptive, having jilted her fiancé at the alter by running off to Australia with 10K of his money as he stood waiting to marry her, she was an ex model who seemed prepared to use all her feminine charms to get exactly what she wanted in life and she was messed up, having nothing and no-one to steady her or support her on her journey. A wildcard, an unknown quantity, and she fitted squarely into that classic *new character* format of *Stranger comes to town and changes everything,* used a multitude of times in classic movies and TV shows throughout history. My instinctive reaction as I read her was pity. Most characters on the show were going to hate her on sight, but as desired by all writers and directors of any character, I, the actor who would play her, was totally smitten. You see I like imperfection. Anything *too perfect* makes me run a mile, I wasn't raised with it, I can barely recognize it, and it felt second nature when it came time to place Nicola Charles on a little shelf in the dressing room, and see the World through the eyes of somebody else. Again just like *Mr.Benn* who lived on Festive Road, I went into the dressing room as myself, and left as someone nobody would expect. Had she been a *good* character, blonde or otherwise, I doubt my contract would have made it past probation, but a troublemaker was right up my alley.

I had never had any problems learning the short scripts of dialogue for TV commercials, and was apprehensive about the

156

amount of dialogue for television characters. As *Sarah
Beaumont* progressed over the years, I would sometimes find
myself feeling as if I'd learnt the equivalent of a small
paperback novel each week. Luckily, at introduction phase,
the dialogue was manageable. I asked myself what were the
things in life I had absolutely no problem remembering *and
why?* Having majored in History, with masses of dates for the
Industrial Revolution and names like *Isambard Kingdom-
Brunel*, along with *The Battle of Hastings* and other notable
Historic eras, I had a feeling I was going to be okay.

Then that night as I chatted with my boyfriends Sister about
this person and that person, filling me in as she often did on
who was who in Melbourne, it came to me. *Gossip!* because
Gossip and the stories told through it were things that none of
us *ever* forgot. We could re-tell what we'd heard *word for
word* at the drop of a hat when unscrupulously passing gossip
on, and so as I looked at the pages, I told myself that the two
or three characters involved were *gossiping,* and let's face it,
they often were.
Before any filming could take place, I was required to shoot
some promotional photographs for the show. I made sure to

stay in character when doing them, and when the photographers said *Come on smile!* I'd say *No. She's not a smiley girl. She's shifty.* They were never very happy about that and it reminded me of being 5,6,7 years old and elderly relatives saying,

Come on Nicola cheer up!

My Australian boyfriend was delighted at the platform my already burgeoning modeling career was now going to have as he was quite literally a Svengali boyfriend behind the scenes. What had begun with the advice about doing my own hair and make-up for the show, rolled into setting up paparazzi photos and more. I remember once it was organized for a cop friend to pull me over for speeding in a borrowed convertible sports car, while we sent a paparazzi photographer to capture the entire event on a pretty side street in Armadale. The photos went global because everyone loves to see celebrities fuck up. We felt like a great team, on the same page in so many areas, except one. He liked to go out and socialize and I didn't. It was the same reason my Grandfather had left my

Grandmother. He wanted a woman he could socialize with, and she didn't want to, so he found someone who would.

It was Day One of my contract with a TV soap opera that at the time was sold in 52 countries Worldwide, and the same episode watched twice daily in the UK by over 7 Million viewers. The first and most overriding feeling I had about that day was that literally no-one would ever believe how *ordinary* and *unglamorous* the set and greenroom were. It felt like going on a visit to see Aunt Gladys at her council house in North Wales. In the greenroom chairs and couches hadn't been updated since the birth of Christ and the uninspiring hallways and communal areas reminded me of a London Comprehensive School, as drafts wafted past me as I walked through empty studios and rehearsal areas, hinting at the Ghosts of inmates from Prisoner Cell Block H that must surely have been loitering around every vaguely familiar corner. It felt incredibly, almost *deliberately* uninspiring for those who were charged with channeling their inner creative from within that space, but somehow, the fact that it *wasn't* intimidating, helped me. In some ways I had gone down a notch. There would be no more first-class flights with Coca-Cola, no more navigating French, or Spanish, or German, as had been the case while trying to order lunch when I was required to live in Paris, Barcelona or Hamburg. There would be no more massive paydays for one day of work, or the need for my agent to worry if I was *overexposed*. I would simply need to leave Nicola at the swinging doors that lead into the studio, and become *Sarah Beaumont* both in front of, and behind the cameras, and the more overexposed *she* became, the better.

I ventured into the greenroom, scripts in hand holding my giant London tote bag that doubled up as my travelling office, with Filofax, Nokia phone and my trusty all-new Nikon F4 Camera, which went everywhere with me. Eyes bobbed up from scripts and magazines as I entered, with most betraying a look of *God who is this now?* A tall red-haired lady with a warm face and piercing blue eyes approached me arms outstretched. Her name was Caroline Gillmer, and I recognized her from an Australian movie I had once seen, but couldn't remember which one. I mirrored her smile and warmth back as we hugged, two strangers having never met before and she pulled back holding my hands firmly and looked me up and down unashamedly.

Well, aren't you a sight for sore eyes. She said.
You'll need some advice on surviving this place won't you!

And she walked me around the glass wall to a small table with four chairs. On the chair furthest into the corner was a large bag that was hers. She said,

Today is my last day. This is my chair. I'm giving it to you! Keep your back to the wall, that way you can always keep your eye on the bastards!

And with that she grabbed her bag, and left.
The eyes of the entire cast and second AD were suddenly upon me, and unsure whether or not she had been joking I moved to put my bag down, as the AD motioned that taking the chair was fine.

Well yeah, welcome aboard! The AD said.

Was I to take her greeting that I was entering a lion's den, a viper's nest? Or was she joking? I was sure in good time I'd find out.

Walking onto the set of *Neighbours* was genuinely an honor. Yes, the walls wobbled, as all sets do, yes, the rooms and houses looked *twee* and remarkably undersized for the business of doing business, but the air was also thick with a heritage and history that couldn't help but breed respect for the success of this operation. Something *so big* was being made on a shoestring, or at least that's how it looked. Having shot TV ad campaigns at *Pinewood Film Studios* in London, on the latest cameras and tech, I was flabbergasted to see old looking cameras on wheels that resembled Dr. Who's *Daleks* rolling around the stage, but something that *Neighbours* had in spades that I had *not* encountered before was that intrinsically Aussie quality, heart. The cameramen were true gentlemen, some of whom had been with the show since the beginning. As I got to know sound and lighting, I discovered this great quality rippled through all departments of the crew creating a spirit of *doing* that I very much admired. They had clearly held this show together for many years, having seen the coming and going of cast and production without batting an eyelid. It felt to me like the show belonged to them, not the generations of acting stars that had sprung from those steel blue sets.

162

I had met many of the *ex-Neighbours stars* in my hometown of London. As a model I tended to be at the same events and awards shows as them. *Kylie Minogue, Jason Donovan, Natalie Imbruglia, Scott Michaelson, Guy Pearce* and more. I remembered the unsettling nature of being at tables in London when one of them had been brought over, their PR people and managers seeming convinced they were accompanying royalty and expecting the assembled guests who themselves were highly successful businessmen, supermodels and British actors to kneel at the God-like Australian soap stars. For pragmatic Brits born with a sense of habitual convention, all the fuss seemed unnecessary. At the time I had met these Australian wonders it was pre-social media, the 90's, where having 2 Million followers wasn't a thing yet. What mattered then was *actual* results i.e. *Did the ratings on the show explode with this person in the cast?* Or *Did this product sell-out when they endorsed it?* It was a money-talks-and-bullshit-walks era of the Capitalist, and when a soap star arrived with this much fuss, they had clearly made bank for somebody somewhere.

As I looked around the grim and slightly depressing greenroom where I would now be spending much of my days

Monday to Friday, I found it hard to imagine that those individuals ushered into London society had such humble beginnings here. It taught me that Soap Stars are a two-sided coin that begged to be admired. On the one side they can be the *grafter,* spending their weekdays head down learning scripts about not-very-much, hardly Shakespeare let's say, and performing them within the parameters allowed on a show that was watched by children as well as adults Worldwide, and on the other they could don a little black dress and heals and walk a red carpet like a bone fide Movie Star, without ever have filmed one. *Neighbours* is often referred to by cast members, including myself as a *Great training ground* for acting. This is true, but what is more true, and most likely what they mean subliminally, is that it's a training-ground for stardom. But there in lies the problem. The immense amount of fame and money that comes from such success is addictive, and the fear of losing it, and the income that comes along with it, unbearable. It is very easy, and extremely pleasurable to go up in life, it's painful and mentally devastating to face one of two possible outcomes at the end of it. One being continued global fame and success, the other being obscurity and poverty, the latter being something I have lived myself, and can therefore speak to. Going from having it all to genuinely worrying if you can pay your bills is depression inducing. It seems almost impossible that someone who lived through years of success on a TV show could find themselves penniless, but it happens. Not in the USA though, over there *The Screen Actors Guild* protects against such financial embarrassment in a way that ensures actors a shot in hell of living a peaceful life after fame. One single pilot episode of a show will earn an unknown actor in America $25,000. Should that pilot be picked up, the actor will be earning anywhere between $25,000 and $150,000 per episode for the duration of the series. That's thanks to the actor's union, who know that an inability to do your shopping without being recognized by fans comes at a price. In Los Angeles a friend who did a single season of Star Trek Enterprise as an unknown actor, bought a house in Bel Air with her salary. Set up for life, and protected by eight-foot-high walls 24 hours a day. Actors in the UK and Australia have no such safeguards.

Does it mean Soap Stars can't manage their money? The taboo of speaking to these issues fascinates me.

And so have a guess *who* my first scenes were with that day? Yep, you've guessed it, the nasty girl who had tried to derail my screen test, only now, she was even more livid. It turns out that her efforts that day had not gone unnoticed and soon afterwards she had been handed her dismissal. That *talk* as she walked away from my screen test must have been quite something, and now somebody was going to pay, and I discovered over the following weeks that somebody was going to be me. Wow, welcome to your first TV role Nicola, this was going to be one hell of a situation to navigate!

Simply put, there are two kinds of working actor, generous and not generous. Generous actors are welcoming of new cast mates, working partners who will need to operate at their optimum level for the betterment of the production, and non-generous actors who gleam pleasure from efforts to try and make other performers look bad or perform poorly. This they do with shadow work, by attempts to destabilize a performers confidence *off set*. Twats we'd call them in England. It always amazes me that such people don't realize their behavior screams *I'm threatened*. I began hearing comments under her breath as she turned away from me in scenes,

Fucking MTA's.
(Models-turned-actors)

Took me a while to find out what that one meant.
Sarah's scenes were initially pretty simple. She would be
browsing through racks of clothing as an ex-model from
London while being observed by the store owner, who was
more than a little intrigued by the new stranger in town. I
remember wandering aimlessly around the set as one would
do naturally around a real store, when one of the cameramen
jumped off his stool and came over. He whispered in my ear
so as not to embarrass me in front of the other actors in our
scene,

*If we're going to see you on camera, you'll need to face
downstage.*

Grateful for the clearly heartfelt advice but still as green as
actors come, I asked,

And downstage is???????

Towards camera.

He said. Rather shocked that I had no idea.

And so for the first weeks of my new career as a television actor I was given a crash course in the physical art of acting and blocking out scenes, not by an acting coach or director, but by the crew, who by the end of week one realized they had literally no choice but to help me muddle through, otherwise they might never get home for tea. There was an acting coach who spoke to me for roughly thirty minutes every two weeks or so, but nothing he said stayed with me. Theories on acting went in one ear and out the other, only practical experience on any subject matter ever resonated with me. Only my own ability to actually listen to what the other actors in my scene were saying, and *re-act* to it made any sense to me for the instinctually emotional side of acting. I told myself I *was* her it was as simple as that. I felt her pain, her frustrations and her insecurities, and worked harder than I have ever worked before to ensure that the efforts to derail me during those early weeks, failed. When I look back at those scenes now it's as if I am watching a different human being. I was both confident and insecure. I could see a determination in my eyes and demeanor that I was resolute in my decision that failure wasn't an option, and often it played out as arrogance. But mostly I can see that I am very much enjoying the experience of acting. Although I know it happened for reasons of the speed required to make that much television per week, it never sat well with me that we weren't able to see playbacks of our performances. Occasionally established cast members were permitted to run off set and stand behind the director as they watched through a scene quickly before yelling *Print!* But for the newbies like me, no such privileges were acceptable as we stayed put waiting for the call. At the time the show was running twelve months ahead in the UK, so despite the fact that I began filming in 1996 I wouldn't be on screen in the UK until 1997! I remember telling my Mother in the UK that I had joined the cast of *Neighbours* and she would see my arrival in a year. She said,

If you've become a porn star just tell me. No need to re-assure me with this story of being on TV "next year".

Thanks for the trust Mum!

Quite why my Mother thought I'd leave a successful modeling career behind in England to become a Porn Star in Australia is anyone's guess.

My storylines in those early months mostly involved scenes with guest characters, notably the man who played my jilted fiancé from England. I'm pretty sure he was an Australian playing a Brit, as his accent was sketchy, and I would soon learn the importance of this from my fellow cast members.

Six months had rolled around almost without my noticing as I learned the business of acting on a small television set in the eastern suburb of Nunawading in Melbourne, Australia, and it had been a baptism by fire. It was contract time regarding my probation. Perhaps if I'd known at the time that Nunawading was the Aboriginal word for *Battlefield* I might have been more forewarned on what was to come, but as it was, I genuinely had no idea whether or not the new character of *Sarah Beaumont* would be picked up or not. I was called down to the office of a Producer, still not understanding the difference between Producers, Associate Producers and Executive Producers for *a talk,* and once seated for the said talk, still wearing Sarah's clothing as the meeting had been scheduled during a filming day, it became quickly apparent that I would be having it with the gentlemen's hand firmly rubbing my knee throughout. Bizarrely, whilst doing so, he talked at length about my being the first female cast member in a long time that thought *logically* and he told me that he admired that as it made me more like a man. I felt the sting of the Misogynistic statement that had just been leveled at me, but understood that somewhere underneath it *he* felt he was complimenting me, despite the knee-rub that was going down. I asked myself if this would be one of those moments, if it were assumed that I would fellate him for a contract, like the stories I had read about Hollywood. I decided to push his hand from my knee in a clear signal that his decision would need to be based on my being a valuable cast member for the show and nothing else. I remember there was a pregnant pause, before he cleared his throat and spoke. He told me that a couple of cast members had *voiced their disapproval* at my being on the show, and that he didn't want to go into it. Needless to say, they had decided to keep Sarah on, and they would be signing the full contract for my agent that day. I thanked him cordially, with any feeling of celebration dulled

171

by the overt touching, hoping to put the whole sordid meeting behind me, when he casually asked me if I wanted a boob job. They were like bombs that just kept coming, reminding me constantly that my value as a woman was at least limited in the eyes of this man. I thanked him graciously like an English lady and told him that as I planned to breast feed one day, I'd pass thanks.

Crikey! I thought as I walked back down the halls. Contract! Knee fondle! Boob job! Geez, they'd been good enough for Marks & Spencer! As I nervously adjusted my regular sized breasts firmly into my vest.

7

It had been a passing comment that had been made by the Producer about certain cast members voicing their disapproval at my role on the show, and to be honest I hadn't given much credence to it. However, the following week, and once it was public that I had passed through my probation period I received a truly shocking phone call. It was from my immigration lawyer, who asked if I could pop in. He told me that the Immigration Department had received a complaint from two cast members on *Neighbours* that a British actress had been given a full-time role with the show, thus taking a job away from an Australian performer. They had also told the department they had complained to Equity. Their complaint had been official, and in writing. Not much shocks me after my childhood, but that did. Luckily, my entire evolution onto the cast of *Neighbours* had been documented with various press interviews set up by the Network Ten publicist and the show was happy for me to divulge that the role had been *written for me* not taken away from another performer. There had been no auditions, no seeking out an authentic Brit, just the decision to write a role for me. Sadly, for the complainers that fact made it impossible for their objections to be considered valid and the entire thing just went away. My Lawyer told me the names of the actors involved, which made it very hard for me to sit in the green room with them every day knowing they had tried to lose me my job. In the end it helped me, because I knew that their hatred of me was serious and they would stop at nothing to derail me. The other actors not involved, which were the majority of the cast, can never have known or understood my hesitation at making lasting friendships or relationships with them. They could never understand how on edge I was every day that another serious attack on my future there may be imminent, and they no doubt made assumptions about my character based on that, but it couldn't be helped. There were two Judas's on the cast as far as I was concerned, and I had to face them, and work with them every day, for years, all while making sure it didn't colour any interactions between characters. I never said anything to them, or confirmed that I knew their identity, but I am reasonably sure that my abject dislike of them was pretty obvious. I can't name them here in this book, because we live in a World where those who tell the truth get sued, and liars prosper, but they know who they are, and if you're reading this, yes, I always knew it was you.

I know without question that the Australian TV stars who had featured heavily on British Soap Operas were welcomed with excited and open arms in the UK, because the benefits of their presence on the shows as a whole would be productive for everyone, yet down under, it was different story, and it began a long and sordid education on how truly vicious and nasty Australian women can be. In fact, my experiences of it would lead me to write my novel *The Witches of Toorak* as I navigated their relentless efforts year after year.

My enjoyment of my work had been tarnished, no doubt deliberately, that's how bullies operate, to make you as miserable as they are, and so I went on to seek comfort and escape elsewhere. My boyfriend was massively independent and focused heavily on his businesses, I had no family in Australia to lean on, and so I got mixed up in the wrong crowd. The five-minute friends, the ones who are just there for the fame, and would disappear as quickly as it did. They got me blind drunk and I allowed it as I dealt with the reality of how unwelcome I had been made to feel on an Australian television set.

It wasn't long before I was in therapy for the feelings of hopelessness it brought me, and I began to question everything in my life as I once again reverted to my childhood and began self-sabotaging. One of my boyfriend's good friends was an actor who had also worked on *Neighbours* Terry Donovan, father of Jason Donovan. He was a wonderful man, so kind and caring, and he set about giving me advice on my life and career. He told me that it was imperative that I save my money, because when it ends, it ends fast. He told me to keep my feet firmly on the ground and enjoy the ride, but always see the bigger picture. The words he spoke to me at his dining table have stayed with me for life, though I'm not sure I heeded any of them, and it was the closest thing to fatherly advice I had ever been given. So when I was invited to the opening of a large Casino in Melbourne, and included in that was a plus one, I asked Terry if he would accompany me. My Aussie boyfriend was filming in Queensland, and I wanted to feel safe and supported on the arm of someone I trusted. I had a black and white dress made couture, which comprised of large images of Dice, and we attended what felt like a Daddy/ Daughter dinner dance. It was one of the most fun nights I ever had in Melbourne, and comprised of two friends having fun, laced with the wise words of a man who offered his advice as a gift to a girl too stupid to take it.

The months that followed at studio saw no improvement in my ability to *trust* my fellow cast members, if I knew one thing to be true, I would never move to see any of them lose their jobs, and so constantly pondered what would drive someone to do that. I knew it wasn't the faux virtue signaling of concern for fellow Australian actors. The pressure by the network to do more and more publicity engagements at the weekends was ramping up and now began clashing with another show I had begun filming whilst the permanent host took some time off. The show was called *Animal Rescue with Nicola Charles* and saw me travel Australia wide to visit with incredible animals at wildlife parks and sanctuaries. To this day, it is my second favorite job *EVER,* my first always being *Radio.* I had to work out a survivable schedule and so I allocated every second weekend to network publicity (which is unpaid) and the corresponding second weekends to *Foxtel* for *Animal Rescue.*

It worked well despite meaning I was working 7 days a week 334 days a year, because *Neighbours* at that time was only taking one month off each Christmas. Often the two complimented each other, with the adorable pictures of me either with or holding Australian wildlife promoting both animal welfare and *Neighbours* simply because my name couldn't appear anywhere without theirs. A situation that remains the same today, and I assume always will. *Animal Rescue with Nicola Charles* worked for me because it again fed into my childhood desire to take risks. I remember one piece to camera that needed to be filmed with Eric, a 56-year-old Saltwater Crocodile that had been removed from the wild for eating multiple tourists in the Northern Territory. He was the largest reptile I had ever seen up close and though he moved slowly, always aware that he was flanked by keepers to stop him should he lunge for an attack, I knew he *could* increase his speed towards me at any moment. The assembled tourists watching from a safe distance behind the fencing that day did nothing to calm my panicked nerves as I could clearly hear their gasps when I entered Eric's pen cautiously. The camera crew and soundmen flat refused to go any further and so with them pressed up against the fencing and me inside, approximately 20 feet in front of Eric I began my speech to camera. Unsurprisingly I somewhat rushed the dialogue, with the director requiring a second attempt, during which I heard Eric growl and let out a threatening hissing sound. As he was in my background, and I therefore couldn't see him during filming, the hiss was a very adept way of conveying his annoyance to me. Animals can absolutely smell fear, and I'm sure I stank up his pen real good that day, I was literally terrified. But that's the thing about animals, we at least know what they are, humans however are much more cunning. And so, I put on my big girl pants on that day and told myself that no badass reptile was going to stop me getting a truly awe-inspiring piece to camera.

I had received word that I had been asked to be the face and star of a new ad campaign for a McDonalds Chicken Burger in Australia, and that they could whip the shoot out in half a day in Sydney. This needed to be factored into my schedule, and finding a place for it was tricky. I was starting to get tired, and was living on coffee and not much else. I can't tell you how much I wanted to chow down on that chicken burger when I held it. Years of watching my weight for modeling and then

TV had seen me *go without* most of the time, and now promoting food seemed to bring it all to a head. The shoot was quick, professional and over with as promised within four hours, and when done I absolutely gorged on Macca's!

I no longer had time for partying or worrying about being seen as *cool* for my profile, it simply didn't matter, because there was no time left in my life for things to get any busier, so I went back to being me and spent most of my down time at home in PJ's and bed socks learning scripts on the couch. This was having a negative effect on my relationship. So as is often the case when relationships are rocky, we bought a house and rescued a dog, as you do.

To many I had the dream life.

A handsome boyfriend who seemingly couldn't take a bad photo, a house we were renovating in St. Kilda East, five minutes from Albert Park and Chapel Street and a successful television career, and yet, I felt something was missing, and the more I went in circles thinking about it, the more the hole began to feel like it was heart shaped. You see I simply didn't feel loved anymore. I didn't know it then, but I am someone who needs an awful lot of it. Perhaps it is the pendulum swinging back from a childhood starved of a father's love and attention, perhaps it is simply my personality type, or perhaps it was the recurring dream I had been having since I was fifteen years old and experimenting with masturbation, that a man with amber eyes, dark golden skin and big lips was the soul mate languishing for me somewhere unknown, and until I met him or knew him, I wouldn't be able to make firm decisions about any relationship. The passion I felt inside me for this as yet unknown figure was vast compared to any feelings I'd had about my relationships with men, but to all intents and purposes, at that point, was just a figment of my imagination. So, when the subject of wanting children came up on the couch one Sunday afternoon, I realized I needed to make some firm choices, and soon.

One of the things I had liked about the cast of the show was their apparent joy when ex cast members found success in Los Angeles with their film and television careers. They would go from not mentioning the persons name ever, to loud recollections of how *wonderful* they were to work with.

Though I was suspicious of their sincerity I always hoped they meant it. However, the same certainly wasn't true when I was offered my first film role in the Australian black comedy *Muggers*. I remember one cast member approaching me and asking,

What? So they're just going to give you time off to do a movie?

What the show had actually agreed to do very kindly, was to schedule my *Neighbours* scenes mostly for mornings, so that *Muggers* could take my TV schedule and move my scenes for them into the afternoons and evenings. I was always very grateful for this, and it was only for a short amount of time, maybe three weeks or so. It was around that time that a Prestige Car company in Melbourne had asked if I would drive around a very cute Lotus convertible for a month, I guess hoping I'd speed and once again be photographed being pulled over by cops in a vehicle only they could supply! And so though sports cars aren't really my thing, I began rocking up to the *Neighbours* set in the mornings in it, and the film set in the afternoons. My first location for *Muggers* was a bar in the city, and the production had blocked off an entire street with barriers to allow their crew trucks to set up inside. As the Lotus crept up to the barriers roaring like a Lion, the film fans and onlookers began clambering for Autographs as the Parking guys opened the barriers to let me park as close to the action as possible. That month saw my life at least appear as glamorous as it was ever going to get, and I secretly loved every minute of it. I somehow knew I needed to drink it in, as there were no guarantees that I would ever be doing a TV show and a movie simultaneously ever again.

The biggest lesson I learned about acting in a film versus acting for Television is that the whole process is massively slowed down. In television I could record twenty scenes a day, in film it would only ever be one or two maximum. Every word, every gesture, every mark was carefully rehearsed and choreographed before the film camera's started rolling. I didn't say it out loud, because how ungrateful would that sound, but it wasn't for me. I looked at my co-star as we filmed a scene at the bar and wondered how fresh my reactions were going to be considering I'd heard him say the same line sixty times so far! I developed a new-found respect for movie actors. The hair and make-up team made sure that not one single stray hair was out of place on my face, my neck or my ears. I was told not to move, don't lift my arm once things had been set, and make sure to not turn my head in a particular direction. It was awful! I secretly longed for the fast-paced momentum of my television scenes that felt more natural, more full of life and instantaneously real, and yes sure, the hair would be less perfect, but so what! I felt my energy levels crashing as the minutes and hours ticked by for just one small and reasonably insignificant scene, and began running Neighbours lines for the next day in my head to survive the boredom.

Some of the other actors could see that I was *green* when it came to Film and began deliberately using phrases and sentences that only *Film* people would understand, then glancing to see if I clocked it. I had no idea what they were referring to, and little interest in finding out. I wanted to go *home,* back to Nunawading and the bitchy TV actresses, the safety of the wobbly sets and rushed G rated dialogue. To the naivety of actors who had only learned their words fifteen minutes before filming them. To the comforting smell of vegemite on toast arriving in the green room from the best canteen food I'd ever eaten, and to a job that felt secure and solid, more like the bank, something that would always be there. The excitement of being a film actor had all but vanished as the waiting and *freezing* and lack of any speed involved slowly chipped away at the joy I should've felt, the joy any human would feel, at appearing in their first movie. I remember driving home that night to my suburban Bungalow and saying out loud as I drove through the twinkling lights of Melbourne's CBD,

I'm definitely a television actor!

But now something strange had happened while I was busy taking every opportunity the Universe brought me, because now my TV show felt I was moving on, and my film career was the thing I would be chasing, despite it being something I didn't really care for. I was essentially losing homes everywhere and I needed to make either film or television my focus. Eighteen months earlier during a meeting with scriptwriters I had sat down with five or six of the shows writers to enquire why *Sarah Beaumont* seemed to be only a conveyor of gossip, with dialogue that often felt like she was being used to facilitate the storylines of other characters and not hers. i.e.; she would often be saying things like,

Oh sure, I saw him walking by the lake maybe an hour ago, and he was holding her hand. I think they kissed.

What was said next surprised me. I was told that the writers couldn't think of anything to do with her, and so I responded with,

Wow really? She's a 26-year-old ex model from London who is single soooooo...

I was told that if I had any storyline ideas for *Sarah* I should submit them to the script department. So I returned to the green room, disappointed that no dramatic storylines were in my characters future, not even on the horizon, and attempted to think around corners so I could gain the character some traction within the framework of the other story arcs that were being woven, and also give myself some much needed experience. I plonked myself down on the chair unceremoniously and looked around me for inspiration. I reasoned that perhaps working with someone I actually liked in real life might be the way to go and at that moment in walked Alan Fletcher. He was always chirpy as a work colleague, diplomatic and cordial to everyone, even when the friction between others, particularly the women was blindingly obvious. He stayed out of trouble, didn't get involved in gossip and seemed to be relatively normal. He was a seasoned actor, having worked his way up through Australian film and television, and so I fixed my gaze upon his gloriousness like a laser beam, and began plotting my characters acquisition of him. Yes, Alan Fletcher didn't know it yet, but unbridled passion between his character and mine was going to be my polarized focus from that point on.

At the time his character of Dr. Karl Kennedy was squeaky clean. My first thought was *Gosh it would be fantastic to turn him into a bad boy.* And so, always believing my first gut instincts to be right, I wrote a short one-page *Storyline idea* and submitted it to the script department. Two weeks of utter mind-bending silence and non-recognition followed with all sorts of paranoia plaguing my mind until finally I was called down to the office. A writer and producer sat next to each other, one on the chair behind the desk, desperately trying to look authoritarian and the other casually leaning in front of the desk arms folded. The air in the room had a strong whiff of disapproval about it, which made total sense when I realized the meeting was clearly going to be short and concise. I was told unequivocally that under no circumstances would the *Holy Kennedy Family* ever be broken up, told through faces that betrayed a look of *How could you?*

However, some months later, and about a year before filming *Muggers*, I had been called into the same office again. This time there was a lot of shuffling around in their seats and I could tell it took some effort for them to speak the words that needed to be said. I was told that the ratings on the show had dipped sharply in the UK, and that something drastic needed to be done to help them recover. I had no idea if that was true, ratings not being something I followed in any great detail. In the end the finer details of the why's and where fore's simply evaporated when I heard the fateful words,

Anyway, they've decided that they will in fact go with your
Storyline idea of an affair between Karl and Sarah.

I felt validated as an actor *and* a writer of at least *Ideas,* and I
was woefully lost for words in a way I had never found myself
before. I had started something on that page, I had lit a fuse to
an idea and it was going to become a reality on screen. I was
told to keep the news to myself and I certainly did. Suddenly
talking about other characters in scenes didn't matter
anymore, because I had my very own storyline coming down
the pipe, although I had absolutely no idea what form it would
take. Then, a couple of weeks later Alan Fletcher walked into
the green room having clearly had something of a shock. He
dropped his belongings down like a sack of spuds on the table
and hobbled over to me with an apologetic look on his face.
He said,

Oh darling I am so sorry. I think your character is going to
have to kiss mine!

I laughed out loud as his face pleaded for forgiveness for
something that hadn't happened yet and said,

189

Yes, yes I know. I wrote it.

But in his dizziness, he seemed to not hear or acknowledge my comment and sauntered off into the make-up room, leaving me to absorb the fact that this was now real and something as a performer I would need to navigate as sensitively as I could, because I had seen what my Fathers affairs had done to my Mother, and I wanted to make sure that all sides of this story were told in a way that saw my character portray genuinely why some women sleep with married men.

8

The pushback I received from other cast members about the powerful storyline I was now going to be one-third of began almost immediately. Aussies have a saying that compares spoiled behavior by adults to that of babies, which is,

Having a dummy spit.

Which sadly is exactly what they had. They said things like,

That's ridiculous she would never go for him.

I thought it best not to tell them I'd had a hand in the storyline idea. The impending publicity requirements around such a controversial story were also ramping up, as photo shoots were hastily arranged of Dr. Karl with his two women stood either side. What I did find strange about that time was that professional actors seemed incapable of separating fact from fiction, and actually began treating me differently for *having the affair.* I was literally *Persona non grata* and I remember one incident as I stood outside the flimsy wooden door of

Lou's Pub ready to enter at the designated and rehearsed moment for a two hander with Alan Fletcher. A female actor *who shall remain nameless (because as you know, telling the truth is not allowed in this new World of ours)* was stood out there with me, as her entrance would occur about fifteen seconds after mine, ideally placing her to see our characters deep in conversation, thus adding to the scandal. As I prepped my *stressed out look* that was written for Sarah on the page the actress whispered in my ear, *I think you and him look disgusting together,* before pushing me through the doors prematurely, making me look all at once, incompetent, incapable of timing and unprofessional. Another actress who was standing behind the crew saw the whole thing and said nothing, in fact giggled. The incident was made even more awful by the fact that the day before I'd had my wisdom teeth removed as a matter of urgency and the entire cast and crew knew that I had been given no time off to recover and was working with a mouth full of blood. I would describe the Actors behavior that day as like marauding dogs, constantly looking for my weakest moments to attack. While cameramen were telling me *you're a trooper,* unaware of the actor's efforts to derail me, I decided mayhem was not what I desired and never told producers or anyone else, simply downing the heavy-duty painkillers prescribed by my dentist and carrying on. Always telling myself that the woes of a girl lucky enough to be on a Worldwide television show were something I shouldn't really be moaning about.

Yet this wasn't the life I had anticipated as an Actor, fielding constant verbal comments from disgruntled actors whilst trying to work. This wasn't like the fawning gratitude and thanks from performers to their cast and crew I had watched as a child during Oscar speeches.

Most days were like a scene from the movie *Mean Girls.* I would often enter the studio cafeteria for lunch alone and receive evil looks from the actors' tables which sent a very clear message that *you're not welcome here,* more *Prisoner Cell Block H* than *Neighbours.* That, to my best recollection was the only time the Producers noticed anything was wrong in person and it caused some of them to occasionally sit with me, which only served to inflate the actor's hatred.

It was strange then that one afternoon, after a long day of filming many scenes for the storyline of Karl & Sarah's affair that I should be the one to run to the rescue of an actress who had passed out after using Speed to keep her weight down, and not just any actress, but the one who had pushed me through the door of Lou's Pub. The human inside me couldn't leave her there alone on the couch, barely conscious and struggling, as everyone else had, her so-called friends on the cast had conveniently disappeared and washed their hands of the situation.

I recalled my own troubling experience some months earlier when I had attended a rave party at the docks in Melbourne called *Red Raw,* and boy was it ever. I truly knew I had arrived in a different land the night I walked through those doors. From the roof, suspended by giant shipping ropes were dancers in skimpy red lingerie outfits. Poking through the groin area were penises proudly on display, accompanied by large silicone breasts at the top. I felt like I had arrived on a movie set, something like *Blade Runner.* The music came at me from every direction despite no visible speakers and the thumping of the dance music pounded through my heart so strongly I thought it might be capable of changing the timing of it. Many of the people there knew who I was and I found

194

myself adopted by a couple who told me their names were Peter and Paul. They were tethered together via large bondage straps around their necks, and they spent the entire evening handing me water bottles and holding back my hair when I threw up.

As was often the case my boyfriend had disappeared almost immediately on entry and so I was used to being adopted by strangers, sad as that sounds. In the haze of the night that had seen me take an ecstasy tablet at the behest of my friends, I was very grateful for the undying loyalty of these two strangers. Then, bursting for a pee I had headed to the bathrooms, which were of course unisex. Once inside and standing in a queue I had drawn the attention of a drag artist who looked stunning, but was hiding a dark secret. She pushed me up against the wall and shoved a tablet into my mouth, holding it shut whilst at the same time clamping my nose causing me to swallow. In the brief moment I had seen the tablet it looked brown with speckles on it like a bird's egg. Once I had involuntarily swallowed whatever it was, she giggled and left.

What followed was the most harrowing experience of my life that saw me *trip* for around twenty-four hours. As you read this try not to judge me or slam me with righteous indignation, if anything I am sharing this as a warning to others. My mistakes whilst a young TV star were no different to anyone else's in the business, people you have loved and admired for years, people who are less honest than I am. It's easy to sit on the couch and lose yourself in shows like *Breaking Bad* and *Ozark* while believing the filth they glorify won't ever touch your life, believe me it does, and it doesn't see you gorge on the shows any less.

The tablet she had forced into me was LSD and I fell into a dark hole so deep I had the fight of my life to survive it, or at least that's how it felt from the inside. From the outside those who loved me said I was climbing my bedroom walls screaming like a banshee, breaking my nails as I grasped and panicked for a way out of *somewhere*. From the inside I was being hunted along a vast tunnel system, which lead to the center of the earth, by the thing that had obviously scared my subconscious the most in life, the Alien, from the movie of the same name. It was so real I could even smell the creature's breath. When I finally began seeing *real* things, my bedroom, my boyfriends face and the curtains which had been drawn to keep the room cool for me amidst the heat of an Australian day, it was twenty-four hours later, and I had absolutely no idea how I had gotten home. Vast amounts of uncomfortable moments followed that evening. Police reports, rape kits and HIV tests that went on for weeks on end ensuring that my being forcibly *spiked* was the only crime that had occurred that night.

And so, as I sat holding the frail and boney hand of an actress on the green room couch, waiting for the ambulance to arrive, I couldn't help but have sympathy for her. She was verging on anorexic to achieve a look that actresses like on TV, chiseled facial features, skinny arms and a more youthful appearance, and her low weight made me concerned about how she was going to cope. I realized that I didn't want to be her, ever. I didn't want to ravage my body with anorexia, I didn't want to take drugs for escapism or to keep my weight down, I didn't want to be *that* focused on my looks and I didn't want to be someone so full of hate for other actresses that I would spend my days inventing ways to blight their lives. How could people who were given such a remarkable gift, that of creating a character on a massively popular show become these incredibly unhappy people? The paramedics arrived and took her away. It seemed as though picking up limp actresses recognizable from TV from a couch was all in a day's work for them and they didn't bat an eyelid.

But the saddest part of the whole event was the very next day. I had gone into the loo quickly before a scene to find the same actress stood with another in a cubicle with the door open. Maybe what she said next was a nod to the help I had given her the previous day, maybe it was the offering of a secret she felt she held to help me keep my weight down, or maybe it was my only chance to be indoctrinated into the secret actress club, but she offered me speed. As she did a trickle of blood fell from one of her nostrils. As she scrambled to hide it, I declined politely, which drew disapproving looks from both of them as they now felt judged, and I walked out of there. Suddenly many of their behaviors made sense to me. The nervousness around me, their anxiety levels, the breathlessness and pacing up and down. It was re-assuring to some degree, as I had originally thought that the uncomfortable behavior was something that only happened around me, now I knew it wasn't. As I re-entered the green room an older actress who must have seen it written all over my face approached me,

Were you just in the bathroom?

Yes. I replied.

Never speak about that in there okay? She asked.

Okay. I said.

But I'm speaking about it now, because I do still see her around the traps in Melbourne, and her life became an utter mess, and from what I could tell, not a single so-called friend from the show did a thing to stop it. The friendships I never felt a part of were bullshit, and in fact more baseless and shallow for those who believed they were real than for an outsider like me who was never invited in. And yet still, when she approaches me today and says Hi at events, *I'm the one*

who feels like I let her down, despite the fact that she was
nothing but vile to me for years.

A couple of weeks later I received a request to have lunch at a
venue of my choice with a features Editor for FHM magazine
in London. They wished to pitch something to me face to face.
I knew it must be a serious proposition to sit on a flight for
twenty-eight hours to make it, so I agreed to go.
I had requested we eat at my favorite Toorak restaurant
Romeos. Photos of me with the owners during the 90's still
hang on the walls today and they still have my favorite dish on
the menu, twenty-five years after I first ate it. *Romeos* always
reminds me of a restaurant from a gangster movie like
Goodfellas as large mirrors hang at the far end, making sure
than even with your back seated to the door, you could always
see who was coming in. I sat down with the very British
looking man, standing out as he did from the suited and
booted Melbourne businessmen in their designer suits. He was
in jeans and a black T-shirt, very unassuming for a man with
such an interesting job, as I was casually stuffing down my
favorite dish of Chili Chicken, not expecting to hear anything
too earth shattering. He sat fascinated at my hunger and haste,

in fact so much so, that later on, in the magazine his first words in the article would be *Nicola Charles is chowing down* because let's face it, an actress on television *eating lunch*, well that's big news!

Don't believe me? Read the article.

He said,

Thank you for meeting me, Nicola. I have some very important news to share with you. Our readers have been voting for months on our posed question of "Who is the Sexiest Woman in the World?" We didn't make any suggestions and simply took our lead from our readers. They voted by mail, so actually had to make a real effort to be part of this, and the incredible news is, that well, they have voted YOU the Second Sexiest Woman in the World.

I stopped chewing and put down my fork, and with Chili Chicken that takes a lot of effort.

They did what?

Yes, he continued. *And we are talking tens of thousands of votes.*

I took a slug of my cheeky lunchtime Pinot Grigio and eyed him curiously.

I don't know what to say. What does it mean?

Well, he went on, *it means you have a very solid male following in the UK and it also means that I am here to officially ask you if you would like to be the Cover Girl for the entire competition issue. You see Jenny McCarthy from the USA, who is on MTV actually came 1st, but we can't shoot with her, she's too hard to get to, and we don't want to use stock shots. Soooooo as you're our very own British girl, we would very much like you to do it, nude if possible?*

Impressed with his balls for blurting out the request I thought about how a couple of years earlier I would have cared more about the ramifications of agreeing to such a thing, about how being on a *family show* might see me compromised by appearing on a magazine cover nude. But as my character was

202

now being fully drawn into an affair storyline, I knew that a cover like that, steeped in controversy would be extremely good for business. Good for me, and good for the show. In fact not only did I shoot nude for FHM during that year, in a full-on Nicola Charles rebellion I also shot nude for Australia's *Black & White Magazine* and *oooohhhhhhh* did I cop it from Network Publicity for that one!

The shoot was organized in Sydney, for reasons known only to the magazine, and was shot in a very bright daylight studio. I insisted on a closed set consisting of only the required crew members, and with only four people present proudly removed my robe and laid bare for all the World to see, face down of course, telling myself that *one day* when I'm older, I will look back on this and say *Yes, I used to look like that.* And it's true, the immortal nature of photography in a number of photo shoots captured my young body pre-children, and it is something I am glad I did. But was I comfortable doing it in the moment? No. Especially not when my butt crack was being powdered down by the make-up artist, because I am essentially a shy girl, and so the whole experience required me to very much step outside of my comfort zone. I look back now and feel sorry for my younger self, sorry that I felt the

203

need to do that, or that I hadn't yet found my voice in more intellectual ways, instead being sucked ever deeper into the vacuous existence of a TV soap star. However, I don't regret the lad's mag's one little bit. They represent one of my several lives and they now live in infamy as testament to how hard I tried to *make it.*

Such is the nature of publishing it would be a couple of months before the actual cover appeared, and it tied in nicely with the airing of a very important point on my graph.

The Kiss

It had been a bit of shock getting the script pages through for Karl and Sarah's first kiss. Alan Fletcher seemed flummoxed and racked with guilt that as a man in his forties he would be kissing a twenty-something actress. I however was on cloud nine, knowing it was the culmination of a simple idea that had come to me in a flash in the green room that day after being told *we can't think of anything to do with her.* The scenario of an extra-marital affair I felt was a very important one. My own parent's marriage had ended because of an affair, to be frank multiple affairs, and what I liked best about it was that the character of Susan hadn't done anything wrong. She hadn't neglected her husband, or got fat, or had her own affair, or been a shrew wife or a lazy wife, in fact she very much loved Karl and so was extremely undeserving of what happened next.

In real life honest men have told me that they, and men in general, routinely *Lie*. Reading the pages as the character of Karl began lying to his wife felt to me like we were validating the pain of all those husbands and wives who had felt the sting of infidelity. Whether you agreed with the storyline or not, rooted for either the marriage or the affair, it was still a very important situation to watch the characters work through. We watched them fall to temptation and be flawed, just like us. We watched them tortured by guilt about their selfish desires, just like us. We watched them lie to both protect others feelings and continue their lust, just like us, and we watched them fall apart as the truth came out, as it always does, just like us. Because TV soaps are such an important part of life for a country like the UK. Let's face it the weather is mostly miserable in England, Scotland, Wales and Ireland. We go to work in our heavy wool coats or puffer jackets, drink hot coffee or hot chocolate, race from cars and buses and trains to warm houses and buildings, and at the end of the day we return home to a hot dinner and our favorite Soapies, because the people in them feel like family. We're catching up essentially with the other people in our lives, even though the other people are not real, and they don't have a clue who we are. Admittedly it's marginally weird when you think about it too much, but it's something that has become a British tradition. American's it seems like Soaps like *The Bold & the Beautiful,* where it very much delivers what it says on the tin. Stunningly attractive humans doing the wrong thing left, right and center all for dramatic effect. British and Australian Soaps tend not to do that. The people look incredibly real for a start, so much so that when a vaguely good-looking cast member arrives, all hell breaks loose in the press, but that's what I like about the UK and Australia culturally, we prefer reality. Flick the channel over to *The Bold & the Beautiful* in a British Pub and you'll hear the roars of laughter from Amsterdam. That being said, I find there is a kind of Kitsch camp-ness to Aussie soaps in particular, and it's not always picked up on by the cast when they travel to the UK and do personal appearances.

There is a fair degree of mocking that goes on when soap characters appear in nightclubs and at events, and it seems to go over the heads of some.

But moreover, this utilization of a storyline idea that had originated as a mere thought in my head saw areas of my creativity ignite with the excitement of watching something that you could not see, something you could not touch, something called *Intellectual Property* go from being nothing, to holding value.

The experiment of this, the demolition of a man's fidelity, reliability and character was something unusual to behold as almost an entire nation in the UK rallied behind the character of Susan Kennedy. Later on I would discover that even as a Brit, my character had become very much the enemy amongst UK fans.

And so it was time to get my inexperienced acting head around *The Kiss*. We rehearsed the blocking of the shot the day before, meaning we worked out with the director where we would stand and when we would move, but the romance, the intent, the passion and the drama of the kiss would be something that either worked, or didn't, on the day. We had been shooting scenes around it for hours, what happens before, what happens after, leaving the central *Kiss* scene until the very last. I think that was done for me. The entire cast would have been gone for the day, so the large television screen in the green room that telegraphed the live recordings to the other actors would have no audience, and literally nobody would know what this looked like, until it went to air, not even me. I remember even the crew were nervous and Alan Fletcher ran in and out of the bathroom brushing his teeth before the moment of togetherness was due to arrive. But despite enjoying this pretend story of an affair, I was very much against them. The child of a broken marriage, having grown up without a Dad and being able to recall the sting of being abandoned at the drop of a hat still remained, and so I hatched a plan. Alan Fletcher the actor was a happily married man. Married to one of Australia's most famous faces in news and his wife would be watching this unfold along with everyone else. And so I asked the crew to order me a Garlic Pizza. It sounds nuts I know, and very arrogant, but I am a phenomenal kisser. Wow I sound like an asshole saying that, but it's true, and so I tried to work out a way to ensure this married actor wouldn't enjoy it, because yes it's acting, and no you aren't remotely attracted to the person in real life, but you are making physical contact. It no doubt broke every rule there is in acting, to make things gross for another performer, but it was all I could come up with at the time. The cameramen roared with laughter as I downed the very smelly garlic pizza behind the walls of the wobbly set, and one asked me to breathe on him just to make sure the garlic had really set in. *Jesus Christ* he said *you've nailed it, poor Alan.* It was my nod of respect to a wife I didn't know, and still to this day I can't believe I did it.

On an emotional level the scene was easy for many reasons. Number one mantra was, portray the pain and betrayal of this scenario like your life depends on it, because the lives and futures of other people watching may be affected by this. Number two mantra, be a good actor *always* be a good actor. Number three mantra, don't be affected by any comments or bullshit on set, stay focused on Sarah and her need for Karl. Despite being something of a comedian on radio and during speeches, I wasn't able to use comedy on the day we filmed

The Kiss, I didn't want to. This was serious stuff, and so I paced, slightly away from Alan and with my back to the cameras, psyching myself up, welling up tears for Sarah's big moment. It was a lot easier than I had anticipated, because yes I am nuts, and yes, I can absolutely tell myself this is real. I used many memories from my own life to draw from my emotional *well,* and I could feel it rising within me, as a lifetime of heartache was pulled kicking and screaming from the depths within me, even as I listened to the director preparing and even as I stared into Alan's nervous eyes. I asked myself,

What if he were the love of my life? Would I fight for him? Would I drag him from a happy marriage? Would I do this?

Yes, was the resounding answer that came back to me, yes I think I would, because when push comes to painful shove, we all do what's right for ourselves. The answer conflicted me, surprised me and got me thinking about the survival instinct that dwells in all of us.

I felt sudden closeness in the moment, as I found the sweet spot between reality and fiction. A myriad of thoughts raced through my inexperienced mind.

Is this what prostitutes feel like? Having to touch strangers? Is this what it's like for girls who go home with men they don't know for one-night stands? Is this what it feels like for all actors? Can he smell my garlic breath?

And then suddenly it was upon me and I heard the word that would begin a change of course in my career at least from that point on.

Action.

Sarah was in pieces, doubting herself after yet another failed relationship. She was falling apart, alone in the room with a friend she trusted, a dear friend, a boss, a *yep you guessed it* a Neighbour. Should she fall into him? Would he catch her if she fell? And just like that, he did. The man, the actor, held her like it was real. Confusion ran riot in my head, all at once I was questioning everything, is it me? Is it her? What's happening? It's really something when you do actually achieve the goal of allowing your conscious mind to fall into a character and become immersed, and as Sarah found her way into my consciousness and she glanced upon her friend Karl through what was then layers and layers of tears, she absolutely meant to move their relationship from friendship into something sexual. It was all there in his eyes, Karl gave Sarah exactly the signals she needed, betraying his own vulnerabilities, and so she kissed him, because in that moment they both needed it.

The seconds of a kiss felt like hours until a gleeful sounding director, knowing he had nailed a massive pivot in a story arc, gently said,

Aaaaannnnnnnd Cut. Got it. Fantastic work guys

As I pulled away from the scene, the actor, the character, I was instantly Nicola Charles again, and wiped away the tears of a girl I hoped I would never be like, had convinced myself I *could* never be like, not for any man, ever.

Oh I had popped my cherry that day.

Not by kissing Alan Fletcher/ Karl Kennedy, but by being the thing I wanted to be more than anything, a believable and competent *Actor*. To nail the job I was being paid to do. Neither I, nor Sarah ever won or got nominated for any awards for the Affair storyline, and I nor she needed them. I had done my best work that day. The girl from FHM and Loaded Magazine who had started life in a Sprite TV commercial in the UK was acting in a prominent storyline on a soap opera that filmed 17,008 kilometers from her home in Worcestershire, and my role was the only accolade I needed.

When the Karl/ Sarah kiss episode aired my entire life changed. I could never have anticipated the level of hate that would be levied at Sarah, and with fans not always acknowledging the difference between the actor and the character they play, they succeeded in letting me know all about their anger. Righteous indignation fueled their every interaction with me and I found myself defending the imaginary decisions of this imaginary character. I remember being home for Christmas soon after the affair storyline really ramped up in the UK. I had dared to anticipate a warmer reception, perhaps some national pride from Brits that a British actress was doing so well on a show that was so quintessentially Australian, but the UK didn't seem interested in anyway. Ramsay Street it seemed wasn't Hollywood, and there would be no cries of,

Look at our girl go over there!

It was Christmas Eve and I had been into Harrods basement to buy a Christmas Pork Pie to take home to Worcestershire for my family and some aged Malt Whiskey for my stepfather. I knew that heading up into the Fashion department would be a costly mistake for me, and so trying to stick to a budget I raced outside into the flurries of light snow to run up to Harvey Nichols and a little make-up purchase from Mac. The street was bustling with Christmas shoppers as giant green Harrods bags full of gifts banged into my legs as I made my way through the Knightsbridge crowds, beneath fairy lights swinging in the chilly breeze. Suddenly I heard yelling and turned to see what all the fuss was about. An angry looking woman of around fifty glared at me red faced and I'm sure I saw steam appear from her ears. She raised her arm and pointed at me like Donald Sutherland in *Invasion of the Body Snatchers* and screamed,

YOU! Leave Susan Kennedy alone! And keep your hands off him you slut!

She then proceeded to clear her throat and spit in my direction as I stood there in shock at the uninvited aggression. As if in slow motion I watched the spit fly through the air and land on my boot as someone she was with managed to drag her away like a rabid dog. A lot of things went through my mind in that moment, as the assembled shoppers looked at me in disgust believing she was talking about a real scenario. Firstly, that I must have done a hell of a job as Sarah for her to believe that the characters behaviors were mine, and so patted myself on the back for that, another was a sort of morbid surprise and fascination, because clearly Sarah, the single female in the three-person storyline, was getting the blame for the entire thing. I got to thinking about all the affairs that had touched my own life, and if I felt the *other woman* was always to blame. The answer was No, because no man can be stolen, he has to *want* to go, and yet, this character of Karl Kennedy seemed to be Teflon. *He* was the one that was married. *He* was the older man. *He* was the one who was unavailable, and yet *he* bore very little blame for it with the majority of viewers. *Misogyny!* My brain cried. *Blatant Misogyny!* It was like being back in childhood. My Brother could do no wrong, because he was a *Boy*. Everything was always my fault, and I began thinking about it endlessly during my Christmas break. I thought about the ways we talk to children, and how it can affect who they become. Mother's who always make excuses for their Sons behaviors by saying things like *Boys will be Boys!* Almost validating it. Girls were never told such things, oh no, we were told to be *Seen and not heard!* And to this day that awful tradition remains for many. Women are judged and blamed and vilified based on their looks, their decisions and woe-betide any woman who speaks out or has an overt opinion, then like me you are labeled an *Outspoken Actress* in the press. You only have to read some of my twitter threads to understand that. I may be posting about my political concerns but still men will say *I prefer it when you are just being a honey badger,* immediately attempting to invalidate my opinion with their giant dollop of misogyny. Here we go again

216

I thought… a little girl is going to get the blame for the entire debacle. I pictured millions of little girls standing silently beside me, also facing the same twisted justice. When *do* men get the blame for their behaviors exactly? Luckily the character of Susan Kennedy made sure Karl knew exactly who he had let down, and promptly smashed him one in the face, and while doing so said a line that haunts women the World over,

I believed everything you ever said to me.

And there it was, the pinnacle of the arc.
Because don't we all believe when we love someone?

My trip home for Christmas then went from bad to worse. The hotel I was staying at in Holland Park had a criminal in their midst, unbeknown to both them and I. My American Express card had been double swiped, and so while I was busy keeping to a budget, someone in an Irish Pub in Covent Garden was removing hundreds of pounds a day, until it totaled 27,000 pounds sterling from my American Express card. I was oblivious until I got back to Australia, and felt doubly foolish

217

when I remembered the moment it had happened. The bus boy had recognized me and had gone overboard on the fawning and fan-girling as I was checking in. My stupid ego had lapped it up while the little shit was daylight robbing me under the desk. Luckily the lovely people at American Express take no prisoners and he ended up in jail. The thief had done me one big favor, he had taken the last chunk of cash from my card on a date when I was back home in Australia and filming, meaning I wasn't responsible for any of it, simply couldn't have been. Phew. I still have the bill from that short three-week visit that saw me robbed and spat on in the street in the country I grew up in. I spent 3,000 pounds on Christmas shopping and clothing, quite a hefty sum for me, but added to the theft my monthly bill arrived at just over 30,000 UK pounds sterling, heart attack material. I cut up my card that week. Sorry American Express, it was fun while it lasted.

I had gone home for a quiet Christmas in Worcestershire with my family, more than convinced I would arrive back to a blaze of glory, interviews on the BBC! National pride at my being the only British character on their beloved Neighbours and a well-earned rest. Instead, I got robbed and spat at on the street of my beloved London. Playing Sarah Beaumont hadn't quite had the reaction I was expecting, but Mum was pleased when we paid for our shopping in Tesco and the teller said,

OMG Sarah it's you! Why are you in England?

To which my Mother answered proudly,

Because she's my Daughter and it's Christmas.

That rare moment between her and I meant the World to me. It was proof. I hadn't run off to Australia to become a *Porn Star*!

9

It was contract time.

I had spent years playing the role of Sarah Beaumont. I had played her well, and she was extremely popular. The main purpose of the storyline, to increase viewer numbers in the UK, had been achieved, with audience numbers climbing sharply from approx. 7 Million viewers a day to approx. 11 Million. She had successfully leveled the holy Kennedy Family, but where would the character go from there? Unbelievably I got the same response from the script department I'd had prior to the storyline, *we're not sure where to take her from here.* I think in that moment I gave up fighting for Sarah Beaumont. I had shown Producers what I was capable of after a baptism by fire as a non-actor joining the show, I had endured the relentless amounts of bullying and being made to feel unwelcome on the show by some of my fellow cast members, enduring it like a champ, never complaining, never taking my concerns to the press, I had completed my first movie playing the role of *Belinda* the University receptionist with Nymphomania in Australian black comedy *Muggers* and I had hosted *Animal Rescue with*

Nicola Charles for *Foxtel.* I had presented an Award at the *Logies* and another at the *AFI's* alongside *George Lucas* of Star Wars fame. I was an ambassador for four Australian charities and had bought my own home in St.Kilda East, and so when a new contract was offered for three more years on the show, I fell into autopilot as I heard myself use the *ONLY* power any performer has, the power to say *no,* and I declined it.

The following day I was told that I would be lunching with the Producer and the Executive Producer at a fancy Greek Restaurant near the studio. Their faces said much without words. They were there to negotiate a deal for me to remain on the show. They offered to double my salary, to an amount I am sure no-one is paid to this day, and I have to admit I was tempted. In all honesty I didn't want to go, but also needed to feel valued. I needed to feel challenged as an actor, that the journey of this incredible character was mapped out and defined, with a clear destination following what had taken place between Karl and Sarah, but no-one seemed able to tell me. I let them speak, which was mostly about the financial offer before I asked the question I had long needed an answer for.

Is she going to get him?

We're not sure yet. They clambered over each other to say in unison.

I don't want to spend another two years floating around servicing other characters storylines. I said.

There is always a little of that. One replied.

They asked me to sleep on it, and I did, but the following day I told them I wouldn't be returning. I have never been driven by money, despite earning a fair amount of it. It was just that *Neighbours* was beginning to feel like a bad marriage, with me needing more, and them not being able to meet me halfway. My favorite word in the English language is *Traction.* Having delivered on the affair storyline I felt Sarah had delivered a lot of it for the show, and I wanted her to get her own house, her own family and a place on the iconic show she had helped bring back to life, but she was clearly about to float back off into character obscurity. I didn't want that for her, and decided going out on a high was the better option. Of course I felt sad that I needed to leave such a big part of my life behind, but I genuinely believed better things were going to come, and anyway, it wouldn't be my life without a large dollop of self-sabotaging.

It was my last day on set.
I don't know quite what I was expecting from the people I had spent years working with but it definitely wasn't what I got. The crew, were awesome and gave me big goodbye hugs and wished me well. As for the cast, the last thing I remember about leaving the show *that time* was the song some of the female cast members sang as I packed up my scripts and phone in my bag for the last time in the green room. One of them being the cast member whose name was firmly attached to an official complaint to the immigration department. It was a joyous rendition of,

Hey-ho the Witch is dead
The Witch is dead

The Witch is dead
Hey-ho the wicked Witch is dead!

From the Wizard of Oz.

You wouldn't be hearing about that effort at the Oscars.

London

Upon my return to London, I was swamped with meetings and photo shoots. Sarah from *Neighbours* was back in town and this time there was traction following the storyline and I felt sure that opportunities would arrive for me. The first omen should have been the address of almost 100% of people who met me. They'd say things like *Oh I've never seen Neighbours* and then ten minutes later ask *Sarah what would you like to drink?* I quickly realized that Nicola Charles barely existed, only Sarah did, until one day a casting director said the fateful words after yet another failed audition process, *I fear you may be type-cast, they simply can't see you in the role as you are so recognizable as Sarah.* It was then I began to worry because the failed audition process had been for the British

TV Police drama *The Bill* and the show was under the same Production banner as Neighbours so if they didn't want me, then no-one would. My dream of becoming a badass British copper dashed before it had even begun. I then audition for the US movie *Along Came Polly*. I remember the casting director joking,

Well, now they get to choose between the girl from Friends and the girl from Neighbours.

I was in no way surprised by which show won that battle.

During my downtime I had begun writing as a creative outlet. Not books or screenplays this time, but songs. Though I didn't consider myself a singer I definitely considered myself a songwriter and had dreams that one day somebody with a real voice would sing my songs and make me fabulously wealthy. Wouldn't that be nice? During that time everyone around me in London was doing huge amounts of drugs, predominantly cocaine. They used it as casually as drinking a glass of wine and I sat at many a table in restaurants that saw sumptuous steak meals arrive and never be eaten, because prior to the service everyone had snorted coke in the bathroom and subsequently lost their appetites. The wasted food on tables that year was horrifyingly criminal. *THAT'S* how literally everyone was thinner than me! It seemed as though I were surrounded by the kind of friends who would be there through thick and thin. There were Lords, Movie Stars, Supermodels, Television Hosts and Billionaires all vying for my friendship and attention, keen for those oh-so-flattering press photographs leaving venues under a rainy London sky with *Sarah Beaumont* from *Neighbours*. But somewhere deep inside I knew that their friendship and yearning for my company was insincere, I just chose to tell myself it was genuine. I was rapidly becoming just a novelty photo opportunity and often it made me sick to my stomach.

Then one of the friends introduced me to an Australian Music Producer who was working for a large UK/ Australian label at the time. He listened to a track I had written called UFO's. I had based the lyrics around my frustrations with all the people I knew in London at the time, and as a first attempt at lyrics it wasn't bad, just a little disjointed and they went like this.

UFO's by Nicola Charles

I see new faces on TV
I see them in my minds eye
I hold my chest but I can't breathe
I want to talk but don't try
I walk along this crowded street
The coffee bars are buzzing
I think the next time we might meet
It's when you're out there hustling

(Chorus)
Coz I am Sad
And I am Alone
And I am Mad
And I am Crazy yeah
You should stop chasing UFO's and see me
I watch you take your life apart
I know that you are bleeding
You were so angry from the start
And now you're busy needing

What happened next saw me have the most fun it's possible to have within a twelve-month period, and for that I will always be grateful, however it cost me dearly on two fronts. The Producer, who shall remain nameless as he is still successfully working away in the music business and doesn't need my failed attempts at a music career to tarnish his achievements, felt like a Brother, someone who's company I was extremely comfortable in. I was signed to a Music Publishing deal which still stands to this day and a half-million-dollar contract to produce an album with a UK label. I set about writing a list of songs, which included,

Chill out Spooky –
A song about a situation in the UK at the time where the British government were closing all the Mental Health facilities, meaning those with mental health issues were wandering the streets and sitting alone on park benches talking to strangers, and I found it very upsetting.

Bitchin' –

I'm a Sin –

The Color Red –

And more

Initially things went really well. I was produced out of the
Pink Floyd houseboat on the river Thames, which was one of
the last remaining analogue studios left in London. This was
to create that fatness of sound synonymous with guitar-based
rock of old. However, once completed the Production side of
the music was considered too dated by the label and so they
flew us both to Los Angeles for a remix with legendary
Producer Chris Lord-Alge who produced albums for US band
Hole among others. Taking the mix to Los Angeles was tough.
I had been moving around studios in London as tweaks had
occurred and during one such week I had begun a brief
relationship with the lead singer of what would become a
phenomenally successful UK band, though they weren't at the
time. Both of us were on a break from our respective partners
at the time, which became our talking point, but neither of us
wanted the relationship to be anything public. It would have
been front page news for all the wrong reasons and very much
detracted from the music we were both creating. It was an
emotional affair, barely physical and was like finding a friend

with the same interests. His career went on to be stratospheric and our time together will forever remain a private but special memory.

During the trip to Los Angeles, I ate lunch with *Randy Jackson* and discussed the direction my career would take. I would have dinner with Chris Lord-Alge at a restaurant famous for it's Italian gangster customers to discuss the mix, all accompanied by my Australian Producer. Oh geez the food was so good there, even though I did shit my pants each time the door of the Italian Restaurant swung open and new diners walked in, just in case one was a Tony Soprano type. To any sane artist they would believe that their career in music was well on its way. Then something happened that derailed me suddenly and unexpectedly. I was asked to do a movie in Scotland. It was low budget and edgy, with a phenomenal script. I had written and recorded my songs, and we were only in the process of remixing them when the offer came in. As I was under contract I went to the label head and asked if I could take three weeks off to shoot the film, as it's release could prove beneficial to the album. I found myself hit with a massive wave of anger and resentment and was told,

Choose! You're either a recording artist or an actor! Which is it?

It was nothing like *Neighbours* who had actively helped me squeeze in my first film despite the extra scheduling work it would cause them. This seemed totally unnecessary and counterproductive. I was heartbroken, and at that time had worked on my album for a solid eighteen months and so couldn't walk away. Reluctantly I declined the offer of a role in the movie with a heavy heart and a feeling of foreboding, which I am often cursed with when making decisions, and walked away.

Of course it went on to be Oscar Nominated.

Then, four weeks later, and after a stella Chris Lord-Alge remix of my album *Listening in Color* was complete, I was invited to lunch with the owner of the UK label at a fancy Chelsea restaurant expecting to be told a projected release date. Instead, an odd meeting occurred, the kind that quickly gave me a familiar feeling I didn't like, one where a man in power was going to enjoy wielding it.

231

He told me that though my album was *epic* and had a chance at being one of the most memorable guitar-based rock albums by a female artist in the UK ever, he had some bad news to deliver. He told me that he had been offered 80 Million pounds sterling for the business and he was selling up, that the label was only keeping their top two established bands on their roster, and I was being dropped. I had already received a decent amount of funds from my contract and so even as he said the words I couldn't believe or absorb the reality of it. I could see that he held no guilt about it happening, or any sympathy for so much work being tossed away, and I simply went numb. The unthinkable had happened, I had lost it all, my TV career, my chance at a second movie to get me on my way, and now I had lost the thing I had worked hardest on, music.

As a teenager I had a nickname given to me by a close friend. It was, *SWITCH*

Because she had noticed that when I am done with a person or a situation, I walk away with such finality that it's as if I had turned off a switch. As I watched him jovially pay the restaurant bill having just demolished my hopes and dreams, I felt my inner switch go off. I know he saw a change in me instantly because he became briefly uneasy and made me a rash offer to buy the recordings from him, for 1 pound, which I did. The Dats sit in a box on the top shelf of my Sons wardrobe. I haven't even looked at them for years because the last time I did the labels on the boxes that read *Nicola Charles – Listening in Colour* made me cry. I learned a valuable lesson that day about trust, business and the importance of taking care of myself before anybody else. I also learned never to trust a word anyone in the music industry said to me again. I only ever took one more meeting with regard to my music career. I'd been asked to meet with Simon Cowell when he was an A&R guy at BMG Records in London. I actually really liked him when we met, as he seemed more honest than most in the industry, which went on to serve him well. He told us that he was about to start a TV talent search show and that when he wrapped up filming we'd talk again. The rest is history.

Luckily, I didn't wait around. I was out of there. For me music, song writing, all of it was gone. I resented having wasted so much time, and vowed to never entertain music as a career again.

However quietly and without fuss I did play around privately with music, and I wrote a song that I still love today called *MANIFIQUE* which sits happily bothering no-one on Youtube under the artist name *NIX NIX*. I wrote it for my children, and the words are a message to them. I didn't need to release my music after all, I just kept it as a hobby.

10

Climbing out of the emotional hole I had fallen into was one
of the hardest things I have ever done. I had gone from Hero
to Zero in two short years and an unfamiliar feeling began
creeping in. Desperation. I am proud of how I emotionally got
through that time in my life. A lesser person would have
buckled under the reality of losing it all.

My agent in London felt directionless and I hated having to
rely on the competency of another person to dictate how and
when I entered relevant rooms. I accepted minor roles in
daytime soap operas in the UK like *Doctor's* and went on
endless rounds of auditions for musicals, something I had no
experience in. I guess this was because of my foray into
music. I failed at the audition for *Chicago* and didn't enjoy
being judged on my dancing abilities and not acting. I sang at
ten callbacks for a Ben Elton musical that included Rod
Stewart songs *(which for some reason I seemed able to sing)*
that also went nowhere. Please understand, I in no way want
you to feel sorry for me, this was all contributory to who I

became, a more humble person, a more driven person, a better human.

I began surviving on voice-overs, and found them surprisingly rewarding. There was acting involved, and voice acting is a unique and interesting medium. There was *selling* and the art of persuasion, which I loved, and there was money, lots of it. I voiced ads for The Observer Sports monthly, Aus Travel, L'Oreal, Alpha Telecom and more, and continued strongly with those even when I discovered I was pregnant with my first child. Bizarrely since moving to Australia voice agents *don't want to represent me* here and that became another very tough reality upon my return.

Wanting to be a Mother.

It's a tough one to describe. I definitely think it's catching, like a cold. *Warning to all women,* spend too much time in the company of babies and you *will* want one. A friend at the time had recently had an adorable baby Boy. She needed help with childcare during a work trip to Paris, and as I knew the city well, and wasn't working at the time, I offered to help. It's a remarkable thing to be trusted with the care of something so precious, and the more I looked into his eyes, fed him, changed him and walked the length and breadth of Paris, the more I realized how much I wanted my own. I remember I announced it in the car, and was immediately hit with a no, but moved forward regardless, as women often do. Turns out that when your leftie Mum had put you on the pill at the age of fifteen and you'd been taking it religiously ever since, falling pregnant wasn't as easy as I had thought it would be. I won't go into the personal nitty-gritty of the tests and stress that followed for the next *three years*, just to say it was predictably hellish, until one day I woke up and did something that came naturally to me, I hit *The Switch*. I gave up on being a Mum, and decided three years of trying was enough for anyone, especially coupled with a career that was on the skids. So I told myself that if I couldn't have my own children, I would work with a charity that helped children in need instead.

A few years earlier I had lost my German Grandfather to Leukemia, and though he had kept the majority of his suffering a secret from the family, the knowledge of what he had to face was hard to take, and so when a friend invited me onto the running team for the Leukemia research foundation

UK, that gave extraordinary help to kids with Leukemia, I decided to give it a go. I began my training in earnest, running most days around my local park in Muswell Hill, North London. It was hard at first, I have to admit, and like most people just making it all the way around the park *once* was tough enough. But as time went on and I managed to get into a mindset of being on a mission for something bigger than myself, my fitness level improved. In fact, *Running* became totally addictive. I don't think there were any down sides to it. It felt good to sweat, to tighten up my body and to build up my cardio fitness. Then we were asked to run in a 10k race at Balmoral Scotland, the Queens Scottish estate. I had absolutely no idea when I signed up for it what I was in for. Instead of what I had expected, a stunningly beautiful Scottish hunting estate, it was in fact a giant army training ground with heavy, mud laden hills that made the entire run more like an assault course than a 10k for charity. No fitness challenge ever broke me the way Balmoral did, and as I staggered over the finish line feeling like I was about to have a coronary I knew that something wasn't right. I felt an intense need to rip my clothes off in the VIP tent at the finish line or risk bursting into flames via spontaneous combustion. Onlookers had to avert their eyes as I stripped down to my bra and undies instantaneously and stood there in the middle of the marquee gasping for air. A running mate threw his bottle of water over me, which helped. I barely remember getting dressed, being handed a medal or taking part in the team photo looking like I'd been dragged through a hedge backwards, or the bus ride back to the hotel, where I lay in a warm bath for about an hour, but I do remember thinking I felt weird. My remedy for weird was to frock up and head down to the run after party where one of our coaches Sonia O'Sullivan would speak and take us through our times and announce the monies raised. I'd drunk plenty of fluids after the race and while lounging in the bathtub, so I figured it was fine to do what all Brits do when celebrating, get plastered. We were handed Champagne as we entered the party and I was looking forward to relaxing, when after one sip I felt suddenly sick and giddy. I was assured by doctors present it was only due to the exertion that day, recommended that maybe Champagne wasn't my drink after a run, and handed a glass of red wine. Again my body didn't want it. I managed to make it through the speeches despite the nausea before retiring back to the hotel room on doctors advice where I lay looking at the ceiling and worrying that running wasn't my sport after all.

The next morning something still felt wrong, so I headed down a deserted Scottish road I didn't know on foot with sore feet looking for a pharmacy. While in there I had a funny turn and the pharmacist asked if I could *be pregnant?* At least I think that's what he said, his accent was off the charts strong. Of course I couldn't be, I'd given up trying, was barely having sex and had been training like a maniac for the past eight months, but I bought a test anyway.

It was positive.

I had been six weeks pregnant during the grueling run, and I knew one thing for sure, my life would never be the same again, as the one thing that had sustained me financially for a very long time, *my body,* was about to change for good.

I didn't enjoy being pregnant. I felt like a pincushion for most of it, and as if I had been invaded by some kind of ruthless alien. It was obvious from the get-go that a Nicola Charles pregnancy was not going to resemble those of Supermodels, photographed stick thin with a cute bump. No not at all, my pregnancy made me *giant* all over, even my head got fat. Swollen hands, swollen ankles and legs and tits the size of watermelons. Finally got those! Most days I felt like a cow in calf and as if I might explode at any moment, and I no longer recognized the body I now inhabited. Then, halfway through the pregnancy I was contacted by *Neighbours.* Oh the timing! They said they were filming pieces to camera from characters that had lived in Erinsborough for some kind of Karl Kennedy birthday celebration and that a video from Sarah would *upset the applecart.* They would film my scene in my backyard in London and the record date was set for 1 week after I was due to give birth. Great! I thought. My full fatness will be on display for the entire World to see. Yes, yes I know, being pregnant is not being fat, but sadly those rules don't apply to actresses. Proof positive comes later on…

Where on earth do I begin describing my first childbirth? Wow, it was unexpected. My pregnancy, though uncomfortable had been pretty much standard. Then, four days before my due date I went into labor. I'll be honest with you it was a relief, and as rehearsed I headed to the Royal Free

Hospital in Hampstead for the birth method I had chosen, drug free and in water. Oh God I am such an idiot. Initially all went well, the water was comforting and I was coping, just, with the contractions, but then something changed. It felt as though someone had inserted a large knife into my vagina and was happily slicing away at my insides. Soon afterwards my back began experiencing excruciating pain and then something truly unsettling happened. My baby bump went down, as if birth had already taken place. Both I, and the midwife were horrified and I remember hearing her say words I will never forget.

Oh no.

She raced out and came back with a Doctor and together they insisted I get out of the water. They helped me get to the bed and then began quite a physical manipulation of my now strangely shaped baby bump, which hurt like hell. I began questioning what was going on until finally the doctor said.

I'm so sorry. You're in back labor.

I had read my baby book from cover to cover. Through pages describing every weekly milestone and the back pages that most pregnant women don't want to read, but know they have to, which describe potential *Complications.* There were many, and the very last was *Back Labor.* I couldn't recall the specifics as I was in a lot of pain at the time, but I could remember the book clearly stating that this one was the kind you really don't want to get. They went on to explain that my baby had *turned* in the birth canal. Not so she would be feet first, but she had inverted herself, meaning her spine was now grinding off mine. I began to fall into a well of fear and panic and as I did the pain intensified to levels I hadn't imagined humanly possible. My brain was telling me that we needed to die, because we had walked through the gates of hell and were starring Satan clean in the face. I remember the doctor vaguely standing beside me as I screamed in agony on all fours on the floor, having got down there hoping to feel cold tiles as I was burning up in the hell of pain. He asked me,

On a scale of 1-10, ten being the most painful, where are you?

I swung my head around to look at him like something from the Exorcist and a voice that didn't sound like mine said,

If I had a fucking gun I'd shoot myself.

He yelled at the midwife,

Get the Anesthetist now!

Day 3.

I was still laboring. Midwives were changing shifts and my chart said *Maternal Exhaustion*. My Mother was called to drive down from Worcestershire to make a decision I didn't want my husband to make, and when she arrived the doctor asked immediately,

The Mother or the Child?

To which she replied.

My daughter. She can always have more children.

Things got blurry after that. Many epidurals occurred. A large
vacuum extraction machine was wheeled in. About twelve
people were in the room, all wearing blue bags on their feet as
they sloshed around in a mixture of blood and amniotic fluid.

I was dying.
And from the words I did manage to hear, so was my baby.
Starved of oxygen after being trapped in the birth canal for
such a long period of time, they deducted that mental
retardation would be more than likely, as I heard the monitor
beeping out her heart rate begin to slow down.

Then, like an angel from Heaven a beautiful Russian lady
doctor arrived between my legs as I lay like a broken chicken
in stirrups and calmly said,

*Nicola we are going to do this together okay. You are going to
push, and I am going to pull, and together we are going to get
this baby out.*

I felt my body tear and my baby emerge, with a head shaped
like a cone attached to a monstrous vacuum machine, which

they quickly replaced with a woolly hat so I wouldn't be
upset.

They handed Freya to me as I lay there more than accepting
that death was the next phase, and I felt grateful that she was
alive, and I could see her, before I surely closed my eyes
forever. Yet suddenly as I smelt her skin and watched her take
her first breaths something happened inside me. I began to
fight for my life, to be there for her. I placed her on my breast
and despite the involuntary shaking of my now broken body
she started feeding, which in itself set off a chain of feelings
and reactions inside me that began to re-assure me that we
might have a chance of making it home. As she fed the
unmistakable smell of my burnt skin filled the air, as the
beautiful Russian lady doctor made sure I would be a woman
at the end of it, sewing twelve large stitches into my poor
vagina. I'll be honest it sounded like she was making a
crocodile handbag and I selfishly wondered if I'd ever have an
orgasm again. I owe that doctor everything, and on the day,
my feelings for her were so strong I felt like proposing
marriage.

I knew I would never have another child, I couldn't, right?
Who would be stupid enough to go through that again?

Being back home with my baby was again a blur.
Friends and family rallied around me as I sat in my chair,
almost unable to move due to the stitches and tried to muster a
smile. I was glad to be alive, but felt very much I had survived
something *barely*. While friends had given birth to their
children without drugs and at home on the floor, my labor had
gone horribly wrong, and I was left so broken I had to shit in a
bathtub of warm water as the pain from the stitches may well
have killed me if I hadn't. But nevertheless, I spent the week
resting and healing before doing what came naturally, filming
for *Neighbours* in my back garden a week later.
I threw on a leather coat, hoping to hide the baby weight, and
tried to smile through the swelling that remained for about
eight days after the birth. I felt sure that I could make myself
look *passable* for TV but it seemed the fans felt otherwise.
I had no social media at the time, and so everything that was
said about my brief appearance back on the show was printed
in soap magazines and newspapers. They had kindly picked up
on one *comment* and run with it as a headline.

Sarah Beaumont looked like a Toad in her return clip.

It was just the tonic a woman recovering from a difficult childbirth needed, let's be honest. And it once again reminded me that for some my value lay in just one area, the way I looked. Held to a different standard than male actors, who quite frankly rarely made efforts to stay in shape, I was being, for the first time, trolled.

I suddenly hated everything I had created. I had set myself up to fail, to be held to my own standard of beauty as a twenty-something *forever,* and it simply wasn't going to be possible, it isn't for anyone. So I turned the page, flicked the *Switch* and became a Mum, walking away from all dreams and aspirations about my career, and focusing on my baby. I told myself that aside from Voice-overs, I wasn't going to be remotely involved in a public life until after my child had begun school, and even then, we'd see.

My sudden move away from being Nicola Charles put pressure on my marriage until eventually a joint decision was made to move to Los Angeles, so that my partners career could be focused on over there. I had no idea what life in

America would be like. I'd only seen the inside of hotel rooms in Miami as a highly paid model. This time I would be going as a young Mother with a baby to take care of, and though I was afraid, I decided that existing in a country where nobody knew my face or name would be a better fit for me for a while. And so on November 8th 2005, eight months after giving birth, I moved my life, lock, stock and barrel to California, and hoped that a new and better future awaited.

I couldn't have been more wrong.

Though I spent some beautiful years with my two daughters in Los Angeles, having become pregnant with a second daughter late in 2006, it saw the end of my short marriage and perpetuated my desire to leave America for good. I faced a three-year legal battle to be able to do that and it quite honestly changed me in ways I could never have imagined. It's one thing to face losing a career, it's quite another to risk losing your much longer for, and almost died for, children. The story of my legal battles with the Los Angeles Superior Court are something that have been legally blocked from being spoken about. Yes, that's how bad the story is. I cannot share it with you in print, though no-one can stop me discussing it in person or during interviews, but to this day nobody has asked me about it. Child Custody has become something I am now sadly a bit of an expert on, but the thing I know better than the legal ramifications of divorce for children, is the malevolent use of them as a weapon to punish the leaving spouse with. People who choose to do that without considering the lifelong consequences to the child are beyond contempt in my humble opinion, and I know many *Leavers* facing the same situation today.

(PHOTO: I walked the beaches of Los Angeles a lot as a first time Mother. The children and I spent our days at the Griffith Park Observatory, or Science Works or the Natural History Museum. My marriage was over and I didn't want them to feel the pain I was going through so kept us all busy. Freya and I have had an unspoken understanding ever since. We often don't need words. She knows me possibly better than anyone else on earth, and I her.)

(PHOTO: I will always be devastated that I can't find the original of this picture. Only this damaged copy remains. It was Freya's Birthday and I again pretended there was nothing wrong for the sake of my children. The girls had become my World and would remain so moving forward.)

(PHOTO: Nova was born with a perfectly angelic face on an apple shaped head. We nicknamed her BUDI. Nobody knows why. I made the dramatic but well thought through decision

to end my marriage to her father when she was just eight
months old.)

And so, as I skip three years and move swiftly on to my
Australian return I do so with a heavy heart that I cannot be
more honest with you about it.
One thing I can share with you though was a message from
my new agent in Melbourne. Realizing I was going to be alone
again, only this time with three children, as I had gone on to
have my Son Archie in a new relationship. I had contacted a
large agent in Melbourne for representation and they had
taken me on. I remember an email coming in on a day I was
feeling pretty down about where my life had ended up. It was
one of those moments where life decides to kick you when
you're down, and I think I actually gasped when I opened it.
My agent was forwarding on an email from Inside Soap
Magazine and his message at the top simply said,

OMG no! I do not want you to do this!

The email was asking me to do a photo shoot and interview
for their regular piece *WHERE ARE THEY NOW?* My agent

was of the opinion that it was an insult, as it seemed to insinuate my career was over. Funny thing is, it was, and I had gotten very close to accepting that. After all, I had run away to the acting capital of the World, Los Angeles, and yet made no efforts whatsoever to find acting work whilst there for two reasons, one, I had no work visa and was traveling on an 03 Spousal visa (I'm one of those crazy immigrants that abides by the Law) and two, I was either pregnant or breastfeeding during those years and was certainly not *camera ready.* This had become patently obvious when a friend asked me to guest, unpaid, for a couple of scenes in his movie titled *For Christ's Sake,* a black comedy about the brother of a priest who used the Church to make porn films in. I was to play Mary; the pregnant Mother of a baby being christened all whilst moaning could be heard from the confessional booth. Halfway through the Christening two naked porn stars and a cameraman would unceremoniously fall out of the confessional doors to the horror of the assembled guests. I was eight months pregnant with my daughter Nova during filming and to be honest, if you can even recognize that person as me, you'll be doing well, I was quite literally a whale. Weird thing about LA is the way everyone is referred to as looking like various movie stars. I usually got *Angelina Jolie* because when pregnant my lips always became massive. So the makers of this particular movie kept saying,

OMG she's a pregnant Angelina Jolie!

I certainly didn't feel like it.

And so, I sat and thought about the magazine offer and told myself that if nothing else I could share with *Neighbours* fans the news that I was now a Mum. It was 2011, the year I had been convinced by a friend to join the newest trend, Social Media. I had opened a twitter account and joined Facebook and straight away had noticed fans of the show finding me on there and sending questions about whether or not Sarah would be returning to the show. The magazine I thought would be targeted and give them all the info they might wish to know in one place, and besides, a magazine felt far more my speed than this new social media, which I didn't understand particularly well.

So against my agent's wishes I arrived at a glamorous rooftop apartment in Beverly Hills for a photo shoot and interview. In stark contrast to my *real* LA existence, which had been in a humble family home in Pasadena, the photographs would make life look a hell of a lot more *Hollywood* than it really was. Oh well I thought, all part of the façade of *Acting*. The journalist doing the interview was someone who I had worked with years before and his name was Jason Herbison. It was he that had convinced me to accept the story offer, as I always remembered his pieces were very positive, and not like the more salacious hit pieces that were often generated by the British press. He seemed genuinely fascinated by how seemingly *normal* my life had become, especially as a year prior I had gone on to give birth to my Son Archie, meaning Sarah Beaumont was now a Mother of three. As I sat there on the rooftop with my messy Mum hair, not having seen a hairdresser or photographer for years, and feeling a little insecure, I genuinely felt that this article might be my Goodbye piece to the soap World. I'm sure I gushed about Motherhood before the inevitable final question came.

Would you return to Neighbours if asked to reprise the role of Sarah Beaumont, fans seem to want this?

To me the question was like asking regular people if they would ever like to win the lottery. Of course I would, Sarah had literally become my Life's work. More memorable than anything else I had done, now that the twenty-minute scene of *The Kiss* had become soap legend and the career equivalent of a ball and chain and something that I would dutifully carry around with me forever, and so I answered,

Absolutely.

I fought back tears when he asked me because it was clear to anyone that knew me that leaving Neighbours had officially become *the biggest mistake of my life.*
Then, about six months later I got a surprising email from Jason. He said *have a guess what my new job is?* I was intrigued. He went on to tell me that he was the new Producer on *Neighbours.* It made total sense I guess, as he had been living and breathing Soaps for some time, and his next question genuinely came as a shock.

257

*Will you come back? Can you leave LA and bring Sarah back
to Neighbours? I have an idea for a storyline.*

I don't think Jason can ever have known the heaven and hell
that the request was going to cause in my life. For me to be
able to return to Australia meant bringing my now three
children and partner with me, and the legal and personal battle
to do that cost me my life savings and aged me about ten
years. But all the while I had a very strong feeling I was meant
to be back in Australia and I very much wanted to bring Sarah
back. The land I loved so dearly was once again asking me to
return. Not for the first time in my life the Universe was
screaming at me to get back there, and, not liking Los Angeles
at all, I made it happen. I couldn't have known what was
waiting for me down under. Still naïve and innocent, I was
only thinking of making a living for my children, and escaping
the shallowness of everything LA.

11

On the night I left LA for good I found chaos at LAX. Our
plane had technical problems, which caused us a delay of
twenty-four hours, the longest delay I had ever experienced in
my entire life. The airline put us in an airport hotel until the
following day and I had a terrible feeling that I was never
going to get out of there.

Sure enough twenty-four hours later we eventually boarded
and as I looked out of the window at the twinkling lights of
Hollywood and then back at my three babies sitting in a cute
little row, strapped into their seats and ready for take off I
realized how amazingly lucky I was. I may not have had the
Hollywood dream in LA but I had raised three beautiful
children and I was determined that whatever it took, their
future and mine lay in the land down under. Even at the other
end things got weird, when instead of landing in Melbourne as
booked, we landed in Sydney due to yet more technical
problems. I wouldn't have minded but the airline then tried to
charge me excess baggage for the required domestic flight
down to Melbourne. I went into full Karen mode on that one,

and finally two and half days after leaving our former home in Los Angeles we arrived in Melbourne. I told myself it would be like smashing a plate at a Wedding, and that the appalling flight scenario would mean good things lay ahead.

(PHOTO: AUSTRALIA! Yeah! We made it!)

*(PHOTO: Archie and Nova experiencing their first Australian
sunset on a jetty near Elwood. Our new lives down under had
begun, and we had no idea where our adventure would take
us.)*

(*PHOTO: Our new life down under involved lots of swimming and living outdoors. As far as the children were concerned Mummy was going back to Neighbours and everything was going to be alright.*)

The streets all *looked* the same but Dorothy certainly wasn't in Kansas anymore. Unlike the nineties, which saw the eastern suburbs feel empty and sparse they were now teaming with vast numbers of people and Melbourne felt more like London than ever before. I wasn't the hot twenty-something that would be spotted by Jan Russ for a starring role in a TV show anymore, that's for sure, as beautiful women were everywhere. No, this time my agents told me *it might be difficult.* I began to feel the sting of ageism within the industry, something that annoyed me greatly at the age of forty-two. It was familiar territory, like being a British model again. I had been over the hill for my model agent at 22, and now acting at 42, which I had hoped I could do for life, loving as I did performers like Dame Judy Dench, and yet the industry seemed to be discriminating against me simply because I aged.

The first thing I was asked to do was write a book. An Australian publishing company wanted all the nitty-gritty on my custody battle stateside, and so over the next two months I prepped for a return role in *Neighbours* and wrote my first book titled *Prisoner of the State.* This is a book you can never read, as its release was legally blocked. I remember the call from the publishing house.

Basically this is what we are facing. The person who has taken this legal action and who is named in the book will likely acquire all the profits by way of compensation. Do you really want to make them rich? I guestimate it will sell between 1-3

*Million copies. My advice is this, put it in a drawer for your
kids to read one day and walk away.*

And so that's what I did. It's a damn good read, and very
honest, but that you see is the problem. In this new World of
ours where everything we see and hear is controlled by
whoever pays enough, the truth can be kept from you, to save
the reputations of the highest bidder. It's why I can't and
won't name bullies and wrongdoers here in my book. That
would give them the opportunity to take yet more from me
and my children, as this is how the system works, and bullies
damn well know it. I find that kind of censorship appalling,
but nonetheless it exists and it's one of the reasons I wanted
my own publishing company. Everyone has their own story,
and though it is true that there are always three sides to any
story, yours, theirs and the truth, I sincerely believe, and am
interested in all sides. All the same the people guilty of
bullying are miserable pieces of work who have to face
themselves in the mirror every single day, and what they see is
the truth of who they are, ugly on the inside. That's Karma
enough for me.

I was now facing a return to the show that had made me famous, one that had helped me buy a house in Melbourne and changed my life forever, albeit while being the target of some quite determined bullies. Suddenly I could hear a song being sung in the background as I looked down at scripts for *Sarah Beaumont.*

Hey-ho the witch is dead
The witch is dead
The witch is dead
Hey-ho the wicked witch is dead!

Two of the three women that sang that song as I left the role of a lifetime some years prior were no longer on the show, but one was, and it was going to be hard to walk back in there with my head held high. I knew from experience that if I had been returning as a star who had made it in LA the reception would have been shamelessly glorious, but as a Mother of three who had been humbled by life, I anticipated no such welcome. The storyline involved Sarah working in mergers and acquisitions, with the character charged with acquiring *The Erinsborough News.* The sweet spot being that the deal would put *Susan Kennedy* out of her job as Editor. It was classic Sarah and not a bad return storyline at all, and I relished the idea of playing the part in a way that would ignite yet more Sarah Beaumont hatred across the planet. I saw her as something of a Joan Collins type character, like Alexis Carrington Colby in Dynasty, viscerally hated and too delicious to miss, therefore viewers would continue to tune in. I have always believed this about Sarah. Make her badder than bad, don't weaken her, make her stronger. That's how life really works, wicked people usually prosper, and it would frustrate the hell out of the viewers to watch her achieve her goals as we all sit there yelling,

What? No?!!!!

Literally my first day back on set and certain cast members said things like,

Well Sarah can't remain in Erinsborough now, not after this, no-one would accept it, it has to be a short run.

266

Of course it does, urgh. Some of the old haters began circling me like predators after prey. Of course they were smiling, always believing I couldn't see past their immense acting abilities, erm okay, and would give me back handed compliments like,

You "still" look good.

Funny, I don't recall any of the older actresses on the show ever being hit with *"still" look good* comments. It certainly isn't anything I would say to anyone, but that's just me. But worse was the rather embarrassing way they would loudly discuss other females that had left the cast for *better things.* They waxed lyrical about the shared moments they'd had with Holly Valance for instance and talked about what a joy she was to work with, all the while side-eyeing me to check for a reaction. I wondered if they'd done the same with me after I'd left, however I suspected not. I remember one instance whilst rehearsing in a different studio arriving early and pausing briefly outside the door before entering to switch my phones to silent. I overheard a very different tone of conversation about Holly in that moment, one that betrayed their absolute jealousy that she had married a Billionaire, and I smiled from ear to ear as I entered having heard that rarest of things, the truth.

Carefully and skillfully, they would seek to put me at ease and began by needling and questioning me about various aspects of my life, all under the guise of giving a shit, and of course I tried to keep things short and simple, knowing that discretion was hardly a buzzword in theatrical circles.

However, through it all the reaction from fans on my newly acquired social media was meteoric. Sarah was embraced fully and this time the character would reach an entirely new and younger audience demographic. Like most people I hadn't seen any financial benefit to social media, despite their claims that it's possible, but it was at least a gauge of how many people were tuning in, and their reactions to the storyline. As a performer it was the first time I had experienced the unusual medium of *Drone shoots.* The network had arranged a drone shot of Sarah walking into Ramsay Street and eyeing the Kennedy house suspiciously for a TV promo about her return. The drone looked and sounded like a giant mosquito, and we all know how I feel about those, slowly closing in on me and then zooming around my head at an uncomfortably close distance. I told myself that anything within two feet and that thing was getting punched out of the air. Pin Oak Court felt very different to 1996, 1997, 1998 and 1999, and I could almost hear the ghosts of characters past, as I became all at once strangely weepy and nostalgic. People I had shared such a massive amount of time surrounded by, and yet so few had become friends. My social media had seen smatterings of connections from the crew, cameramen and sound, a couple of directors and a hairdresser, but generally it seemed they had been glad to see the back of Nicola Charles. I thought about my three children, those I was doing this for, and filmed a killer promo that betrayed little of Sarah's true intentions and yet teased much.

I think the thing I found most disturbing about Sarah's first return was that those I did get on well with were afraid to get too close, for fear of drawing the wrath of the bullies in the cast. Unlike 1998 when I was inexperienced and essentially a kid, I was someone who now knew who I was. Someone who had lived through something that had caused a huge ego death within me, and it was unsettling to be back in the company of people who had seemingly had little personal growth in the twenty years I had been away. I was extremely relieved to rush home to my beautiful babies at the end of each day and insulate myself from their behaviors. It was during this time that my fascination with politics began. We all face politics at work and we all live the outcome of politics in our everyday lives, and so instead of falling victim to it I decided to study it, both in human behavior and globally within governments. Politics had always been immensely private for me. I was raised by two extremely left-wing parents, and have vivid memories of playing in the sand on nudist beaches and listening to my Mum talking about *Ban the Bomb*. My brother had been handed cigarettes by my father at the age of twelve and my Mum had put me on the pill at the age of fifteen. There had been little consequences to actions, even when my brother took one of my Dad's guns from the gun closet and shot himself in the face with it on a day he had wagged school. My Dad had developed a weird fascination for the Occult and Religion was never part of the agenda and I had been frowned upon by both of them when I announced I wished to attend the local Sunday School. I *should* have grown up as left-wing as it's possible to get, maybe moved to a hippie commune as my father had suggested and breastfed other women's children! No, I certainly didn't see any of that in my future. I had somehow popped out a little Conservative, and I had spent the majority of my childhood frowning upon my parent's marital antics and looking forward to the day I might escape them. But as I got older, my politics became less and less private. I felt a desire to share them, get feedback and discuss the matters at hand. The echo chambers the lefties seemed to exist in just wouldn't work for me. I needed to hear both sides. It was 2013 and my now very short return to *Neighbours* had not become what I had hoped. I had given the return my best shot and yet as far as Producers were concerned it was Goodbye, again.

I certainly realized that the Universe had one hell of a sense of humor. My partner had no work visa for Australia, and I was now an unemployed Actor with an agent showing great concern about my age and solely financially responsible for feeding and sheltering five people. YI noticed that when I turned on the TV I saw the same actors starring in Australian television shows that had always been there. It was an Australian click, and as a Brit I wasn't in it.

During my return I had hired a Nanny to play with and care for my children while I filmed. On her last day we went for coffee as she said an emotional goodbye to the three children, she'd had so much fun with. I mentioned that I would now need to get a *real job* and she laughed loudly, scoffing at the idea of it.

You can't get a real job? You're Sarah Beaumont?!!!!!!

But I had no choice. It wasn't about me anymore, and so I told her to let me know if she heard of anything.
A week later she rang me.
She told me that she had a contact at a Mercedes-Benz car dealership, and that she could help me get an interview.
Without knowing what exactly for I contacted them.
Just walking through the doors and into the Service Department was agony. Literally everyone knew who I was, and they were more used to seeing actors walk in and buy cars than arrive looking for a job. The cricketer Shane Warne was milling around between vehicles as sales ladies laughed loudly at his jokes. I dropped my head down to the floor, hoping he didn't remember sitting next to me some years before at an

awards show. My interview saw me offered the role of Service Receptionist and I now had to decide how to get from my home in Caulfield to the dealership several suburbs away each day. I had no Australian credit, no funds to buy a car and had spent my life savings on legal costs to get my kids out of the USA and back to Melbourne to film for just six weeks on Neighbours, and so I was left with only one choice, I would cycle to work and back every day. Luckily cycling was a hipster trend at the time, so I could use *fitness* as the excuse for why a woman in her forties who used to be famous had no vehicle to drive. The irony of working for Mercedes-Benz and not having a car of my own was not lost on me. Sometimes I would move the fancy cars around, getting them out of the arrivals area or whizzing them up for a car wash. It often made me question where I had gone wrong in life that I couldn't afford to own a car, not yet anyway.

Over the next eighteen months I would be trained at the Mercedes-Benz head office, mostly on loyalty to the brand and rolling customers into their new *Agility Program.* Luckily, I had scored highly on *Loyalty to the brand* in the required Psyche Test, and the darker side of my soul laughed when I saw the results, as I had definitely answered with what I thought they wanted to hear. Acting was already coming in handy. I should never really have seen those results, but my Manager had betrayed them to me to create a discussion point. As I sat in the unbelievably beautiful cars, I knew I'd never be able to buy one, but I had ambitions of maybe attempting to sell them. However, despite working my butt off for eighteen months in the Service department, was constantly told by the sales team *he won't let you go*, referring to my Manager in Service. So I did my best work, helping the customers of that particular dealership have a smooth Service day on their $250,000 C63 AMG cars, amongst others, and I tried not to cry when they asked me,

Why is Sarah Beaumont checking me in for Service?

Are you researching a role?

Often I would be asked to do the filing by the twenty five year old Service Advisors, who would smirk and laugh as Sarah Beaumont ran around doing the work no-one else wanted to do. The year was 2015, and after working like a demon from the tender age of 17, gracing the covers of over thirty magazines, being voted the Second Sexiest Woman in the World two years in a row and creating the hit character of Sarah Beaumont on Australia's longest running television Soap Opera, watched in fifty-two countries Worldwide, I was filing customer record files in a smelly, carbon-monoxide filled Service Department to feed my kids, but by God it was worth it.

(PHOTO: My new life at a Mercedes-Benz dealership. I was desperate to work up to a role in sales, but never quite got there with the brand.)

That's how much I loved Australia, that's how much I wanted my kids to grow up here and that's how much ego death had occurred for me to realize that when all was said and done, and the dust had settled, I wasn't that special after all.

I began working six days a week, going in on Saturdays for customers who couldn't make it in Monday to Friday, all the while missing time with my kids and trying to save up.
Then, as I sat at my desk with multiple screens open on my desktop, Service bookings, Customer complaints, Vic Roads Rego Checks, internal work emails and my own personal Gmail account, an email popped up from Fremantle Media. I had to think for a moment, because in my old brain *Neighbours* had always been Grundy Television, but then remembered it was Fremantle's show now. In it they asked me who my agent was, because they wanted to send an offer for Sarah to return *again* in 2016 and to arrange for scriptwriters to meet with me and explain their plans for her.
I started crying at my desk, a mixture of shock, excitement and disbelief. My co-workers threw questions at me across the open plan office,

Pregnant?

Lottery win?

Death in the family?

But I wasn't telling anybody, not until I had a signed contract in front of me. I needed to know what they had planned for Sarah and how long she would be back for.

The meeting was held within days, and as I returned to the Production office of *Neighbours* in Nunawading I felt sure that they would finally see the sense in Sarah returning to Ramsay Street permanently, or at least for a standard three-year contract and eagerly sat down with the young scriptwriters to discover what they had in mind. My thoughts were racing with hopes for Karl and Sarah, and a potential future together, and I braced for the news my hopeful heart had longed for, for over fifteen years, but what was said next shook me to my core. I was told that Sarah would be returning with her teenage Son, who was a famous kid from a reality TV show that finds singing talent, at the time very fashionable on TV globally, and that Sarah would be back for reasons unknown, raising eyebrows and insecurities particularly for

277

the character of Susan Kennedy. That Sarah would be dangerously caught up in their major storyline *Hotel Deathtrap* and that eventually, after residents noticing Sarah struggling with a health issue, the viewers would learn ahead of the shows characters that she was in fact dying of stage three stomach cancer. As the words left his lips, I went numb, as if it were my personal diagnosis. I looked at the face of the twenty-something scriptwriter who was delivering the *great news* and wondered how they could keep doing this to female characters on the show. As a writer myself I knew that a show depicting the everyday lives of inhabitants in one street could only make *so many* female characters ill with cancer or another debilitating disease, and so far, their ratio was a little high. One female over forty who was pretty hot and sexy had been given breast cancer, Susan Kennedy had been given Multiple Sclerosis and another was heading towards a death from cancer too. Now they wanted Sarah to battle cancer too? I felt a well of anger boil up inside me as I said,

So all us middle-aged women get sick and die, do we? Funny the male characters don't?

There was a difficult pause before he blurted out,

She probably won't die! In a bizarre twist Mrs. Kennedy will help to save her!

I was torn, between the opportunity of acting the part of a cancer-stricken Sarah, knowing they had vastly overplayed their cancer hand on the show, meaning it would be nothing new for the viewers, and needing a job desperately. Before I spoke, I thought about the people close to me I had lost to cancer in those recent years, my father, my aunt and my grandfather, and deciding to make sure I would play this as authentically as possible as a homage to them. He told me that again it was only a guest role, just a few weeks, and as I realized that my value as an older woman and cast member was now clearly only as a brief publicity draw I nodded my head and accepted. What choice did I have?

I remember going home to my excited family to find three children bouncing up and down eager to hear the news on what Sarah the man-stealing-hussy-of-Ramsay-Street would be doing next and having to tell them she'd be dying. I tried to make light of it for them and told them,

The party is over for Sarah Beaumont

Making sure I re-assured them that not all Mums of this age get sick and die. With a deep sadness I stopped worrying about what I looked like, knew I would never work on the show again after this, and diligently began learning the scripts that would see the final take down of this iconic femme fatale.

I headed back into work at Mercedes-Benz to request some time off, an unpaid extended break for the short guest role I had been offered and got my head into the reality that corporate work was now my entire future, and the filing would be waiting for me when I got back, my colleagues shocked that the return was not permanent. I was disillusioned with acting in general from that point on, with a show that was offering long contracts to female actors from a historically competing show Home & Away, while undervaluing the characters their own show had created, and harboring a fair amount of resentment about the loss of my life savings to

280

return for a role on *Neighbours* that had lasted just a few weeks. Nevertheless, I once again got my head into my script folder like a good soap soldier.

There were a lot of tearful goodbyes during that last appearance of *Sarah Beaumont*. I told myself that as Karl Kennedy drove her to the airport, they stopped off at a hotel to make love for the very last time. It was how I coped when existing inside Sarah's head. But the biggest goodbye was from me, Nicola Charles. I knew I wouldn't play the game anymore, wouldn't worry if I was good enough because I knew *I was,* wouldn't wait for the phone to ring, or remain loyal to a show that had happily not given a shit about a character that resonated so strongly with British fans. That I would answer all tweets about when will she return with, *she won't be,* flick my *Switch* and move on. I could never again accept a *guest role* on a show I helped so much in the UK and with publicity for years and years, and to this day fully expect fans to see a phone call on the show as Karl Kennedy is told,

Sarah Beaumont is dead.

Besides, my marriage in real life was again ending, and I had no more room for bullshit in my life. Only reality.

I remember one emotional scene towards the end of filming where an established cast member said after the director called cut,

You know what Miss Charles; I was wrong about you. You really can do this.

Do what? I enquired.

Act. You were really good.

I had been on and off the show since 1996, had worked my arse off for publicity, losing hundreds of weekends flying all over the country to promote it, unpaid. I had won back millions of British viewers, never let them down or failed to learn scripts, had never caused the kind of vile feelings I was subjected to in anybody else, instead making every actor I encountered feel welcome and respected, but it wasn't enough, because I couldn't control that one aspect, I was getting older in a business that cannot forgive it. I finally accepted that I was always going to be an outsider on the Neighbours set.

I dutifully concluded publicity on Sarah's final return, one night staying up without sleep to do multiple phone interviews with British radio shows, only to receive a scathing email from the publicity lady about why I spoke so brutally about being disappointed with Sarah's cancer storyline on live radio. I had made a move against the establishment, told the truth, shared my true feelings and for that I became the *Neighbours* black sheep. *You really were good!* Felt like a total and unbelievable insult from someone I had worked with *for years.*

Once the ride had come to an end the hangers on and fame hungry fake-friends all disappeared, clearing the way for more genuine connections, even though when they went it was in a flurry of hatred and vitriol. All the same, I appreciated the Spring Clean, and I realized I would need to be valued for more than my ability to tell believable lies in front of a camera, and focus on a new corporate career that would enable me to survive as a single Mother of three.

Most days I forget that I played Sarah Beaumont on a TV show. Only when journalists write about my books and opinions do I see it there and remember, or when I'm shopping and my hair is tied back in a ponytail and the person next to me in the supermarket queue says,

I'm sorry, it's you isn't it?

I bear a decent amount of responsibility when it comes to public sightings and autograph hunters. I accept that my entire life was forever changed by twenty minutes of filming one stage kiss, and remembering I'm British behave in a polite and respectful manner, usually accommodating the fans I do come across. I don't engage in gossip when in social circles, despite the endless questions about cast members and what they were really like. But where I used to view my role on the show as the reason I originally stayed in Australia, and made the decision to come back again, my recent experiences have proved to me that it was all just a convenient stepping stone used by the power of the Universe to get me back here. Not for financial gain, global fame or a continued acting career, but for something far more powerful and life changing, something so turbulent and core-shaking that of course only abject suffering could have brought it to me in true British Shakespearian style.

True Love.

Because life is a pendulum and what swings wildly in the direction of disappointment one day can return you to joy the next. What was coming my way in the land down under wasn't even Australian it was Greek. I waited over 47 years for it, but when it arrived it made up for all the years I had spent alone longing for the kind of love I had never known, from a man, from a father, from anybody.

12

This is where my story gets very personal and very hard. I made a promise to myself when deciding to write this book, a promise that was made after fighting through Covid-19 and after finally finding peace in my life, that I would do my children and readers the honor of being truthful, even if that truth was embarrassing and painful.

While working for Mercedes-Benz I saved enough money for a deposit on a car. I bought a small Hyundai, that after cycling everywhere for years felt like a Rolls Royce. I would often dream of one day owning another Land Rover Defender, having owned one as a model in London, and would gaze longingly at the tricked up black one I was using as my screensaver, much to the annoyance of my Mercedes-Benz bosses. *British crap* they would often say as they walked past my desk. But I had learned to drive in an old 1961 110 that belonged to the father of an ex-boyfriend. The stupid heap of a thing had cast some kind of spell on me, leaving me with a lifelong yearning for them. I'm not alone, it's a sickness, not at all humorous for those of us suffering through it. A friend had gone on to do very well at a Land Rover Dealership in Melbourne and was now the dealer principal, and, knowing of my irrational obsession sent me an email about six months after my Hyundai purchase. He said,

Hi There! So, that Long Wheeled Base Defender you wanted? Did you know they are closing the factory in the UK? I have ONE long wheeled base one left, and we are not getting anymore! It's yours if you want it! Trade price! Let me know if you want a picture?

I immediately emailed back with,

Do NOT send me a photo of that Defender I am begging you. I am in no position to buy it.

Sure enough two minutes later a photograph arrived of a Corris Grey Land Rover Defender 110, and I fell madly and deeply in Land Rover Love. Bastard! I emailed back and five minutes later I was arranging to see it that very evening. It's a strange thing that happens when a motoring enthusiast gets behind the wheel of their dream ride. It's very like falling in love, in the sense that it's irrational and sees you pulled along on a tidal wave of bad decisions and risky choices. I asked him if he'd trade in my Hyundai, to which he laughed loudly and said *for whom? None of my customers will want it!* So I made a decision I will never regret and purchased my first brand new long wheeled base Defender with 13 kilometers delivery mileage on the clock, a car I could barely afford but that I simply couldn't live without. As I drove it into the lot at Mercedes-Benz for the first time, hoping for a staff parking space like everyone else, I was promptly yelled at and told to *get that thing off this lot! The road for you!* I knew exactly why; she was an absolute stunner. A British titan of off-road brilliance, and as she towered above the Mercedes-Benz ML's her presence would never do. And so I parked her on the road, right outside the glass windows of our office, and was often asked about her by customers.

(PHOTO: My much loved Land Rover Defender. Corris Grey 110. She has facilitated many Australian adventures, from snowy mountains to coastal drives and all over the Grampians. This silly car has often made my life worth living.)

I had many reasons to swallow my pride, file those records and walk through the sniggers and the sexual harassment that's inevitable when a former soap star goes to work in an office. My children primarily, the car payments I could barely afford, and the determination that if I could survive the bullies on a television set, I wasn't going to let a couple of creepy men at a dealership end my career. One manager used to walk past my desk daily suffering an inability to do so without saying *something,*

Hey Nicola, would you like me to get you a banana for lunch?

No thank you. I'd respond.

To which he would always say,

Oh please let me put my banana in your lunchbox....

It was as if I had fallen into an episode of Benny Hill and simply couldn't believe that grown men in reasonably prominent positions within a corporation could behave so badly and disrespectfully to a female, all in an open plan office with co-workers and customers listening. But my childhood had taught me that for some there simply are no boundaries or filters. These behaviors continued all while we were expected to attend *Courses* on *Sexual Harassment* where we'd be described an offensive scenario and then have to decide if it was deemed Sexual Harassment or not. None of the examples were ever as bad as my real experiences in that office, but afraid of losing my job and the ability to support my three kids I kept my mouth shut. And so, when I was approached by an outside contractor and offered a job with their organization, I strongly considered it just to get out of that environment. The day he offered it to me I had talked an irate customer down from the ledge, and unbeknown to me he had been watching. She had purchased a vehicle with a hefty price tag and wasn't happy with it. Unfortunately, her modus operandi was to scream loudly like a spoilt child inside the showroom in an attempt to sully the name of the dealership in front of other customers. I was charged with calming her down, and eventually the dealership did the unthinkable and she received a new for old swap of her car. I'll never forget that particular incident, because it taught me that if rich people shout and scream enough, they usually get what they want. The people I grew up around in Worcestershire would never have behaved like that inside a Mercedes-Benz dealership or any other kind, just wouldn't happen. I often felt grateful for not having the same mindset as some of those customers, and staff would refer to them as *Special* with a Spanish accent. To them we were peasants and their every whim was to be catered for, because as I was often told, *that badge* bought them an exclusive membership into the first-class lounge, and they intended to make full use of it. I remember one day walking back from the bathroom to see Alan Fletcher, yes, Doctor Karl Kennedy himself walking around the showroom. The staff were abuzz with excitement imagining a dramatic reunion of Karl and Sarah from Neighbours, but instead there was a brief two second greeting of *Oh Hi* before he turned away. I could see he was embarrassed for me, and so I did what I always do, and made it easier for the other person. In fact, he stayed less than five minutes and I had an awful feeling my presence had driven him away as a customer. After he left one of the Service Advisors said,

Wow, no love lost there then.

He was absolutely correct, and it was a stark reminder of how much I was still considered *an outsider* and possibly an *embarrassment.*

The new role I was offered was that of Business Development Manager for a fleet of Accident Replacement Vehicles to hire out on a daily basis to dealerships and panel beaters for their customers to drive while their cars were being repaired. The concept was simple enough and as relationships were my

292

specialty, I was confident it would work for me. The added bonus was that for the first time I wouldn't be working in one place, I wouldn't be working in an office. I would be driving around in a company car visiting partners and drumming up business. It was empowering to hand in my resignation and move one tiny rung up the corporate ladder whilst escaping the goldfish bowl of the dealership. I will always be grateful for my time there as it taught me so much about life. Like the cars it was a well-oiled machine that ran surprisingly well, and most of the staff were dedicated and professional. What I found most surprising was the response of some of the customers, who wished to stay in contact with me, one, a television producer, going on to book me to host a documentary show for him. I was touched by their affection and glad that my work there had made a small difference. So I took my embarrassingly large Land Rover Defender off the roadside outside the dealership for the final time and headed into a new phase.

I hadn't really anticipated what *being on the road* might entail, and walking into chilly panel shops on deserted industrial estates in Campbellfield at 7am was actually quite frightening.

I quickly learned to dress down and in loose clothing. The tattooed workforce didn't get too many female reps in heals walking in, particularly those who bore a striking resemblance to a television character, and I have to say on a couple of occasions I did feel afraid. However quite quickly things changed, and I learned a valuable lesson about not judging a book by it's cover as I began to feel a warm connection to the workers and business owners who spent their days covered in oil and paint repairing crashed vehicles that to me looked beyond saving. The smell of oil and paint was a distant memory of my father's garage where he built fiberglass fairings and repaired his Norton motorbikes. I've always been driven by scents, and though most people would hate the smell coming from panel shops I felt strangely at home in it. I began selling to the strangest of characters, business owners who claimed to be Lebanese gangsters, Turkish hit men, Biker gangs and a whole host of social outcasts that most never get to meet. I felt safer and happier in their company than I ever did on the television set. I knew why, they were more like me, and they somehow knew it too. They wanted to help me, and protect me, and would recommend my business to their friends and contacts, sending me over for coffees and meetings. Unlike the cast on the show and the sniggering staff at the dealership, the scary looking mechanics and painters would be kind and say things like,

Never mind girl, you were always too good for that show anyways.

Their kindness really touched my heart and I made some lifelong friends.

I often smiled as I heard myself engaging in really quite fowl language and jokes, probably as far from PC as it's possible to imagine, as my British accent slowly started falling, and I was for quite some time content with this new life of selling on the road.

Then I got a call from the Principal of a Land Rover Dealership. I had applied for a Sales job there whilst at Mercedes-Benz when it became very obvious I wasn't going to be allowed to move into Sales. I had quietly taken the interview and been unsuccessful, with the Principal telling me they had gone with someone who had 25 years of experience.

However, during the call, the Principal was big enough to say he'd *made a mistake* and was I still interested. Now I was totally torn. I had enjoyed being out of the goldfish bowl of the dealership and free on the road, but this was Land Rover.

For me, part of the allure of driving a Land Rover Defender is that its not controlled by on-board computers or modules. It either works, or it doesn't, and it if doesn't there won't be a little message that pops up telling you to seek assistance with your Brakes etc, it will simply need a mechanic to check it out. If your legs are getting wet then the roof leaks and if your driveway is greasy, it has an oil leak, and I love the simplicity of that. However, I also held a deep fascination for where the brand was *going* moving forward and why this simple design that had been so beloved globally was now going to be discontinued after 67 years of manufacture. I reasoned that going to work for Land Rover would help me find out, whilst also getting paid. Besides, there were rumors in the Accident Replacement Vehicle industry that Insurance companies had *had enough* of the costs associated with hire vehicles during crash repairs and I felt it might be a prudent time to leave the business.

I absolutely loved working for Land Rover. Despite the endless online training modules and quite rigorous sales targets I found the whole experience very enjoyable. In fact, it was the kind of job I could probably do for a very long time. Sure, it saw me lose Saturdays with the kids, but they were wanting for nothing and my job was secure. I enjoyed learning about the new models and marveling at how high-tech the new Land Rovers were, whilst all the while secretly feeling happy that I had purchased one of the last great motoring designs in vehicle history. There were characters to navigate and adjust to like any position, but the environment and culture were pretty great. I also got to give my Defender a rest most days as I drove the new Discovery Sports as my company car, which allowed me to use underground car parks! Something of a treat for a Defender owner who is prevented from utilizing them due to the vehicle's height.

(PHOTO: Spending my Sundays driving "other Land Rovers" around the Australian countryside with the kids was a massive perk of the job. This Discovery 5 was my absolute favorite until some lucky bugger purchased her as a Demonstrator.)

So there I was bowling along in my new, not so glamorous, but pretty stable life at Land Rover when a couple of businessmen arrived at our dealership late one afternoon. They weren't dealing with me at all, and in fact I was about to leave for the night when one of them approached my desk and looked at my business card. He rubbed his chin and looked up at my face,

I know that name…

I thought, here we go, a *Neighbours* fan, and I prepared my
stock standard answers regarding why Sarah Beaumont was
selling cars. Embarrassingly he hadn't recognized me from my
recent return to the show at all, but instead knew of my work
in the Accident Replacement Vehicle industry. He offered me
a job on the spot. I laughed out loud and yelled across to my
Dealer Principal joking that I had been made a better offer and
would be out of there soon. His face went grey, no doubt
pondering the multiple and expensive training courses he had
sent me on, and tried to laugh at the joke in front of the
customers.

I gracefully turned the job offer down, still believing the
industry was likely to be re-structured by the insurers and
quite frankly loving my job with Land Rover in the sleepy
Eastern Suburbs of Melbourne. But these guys weren't giving
up that easily, they offered me first the Head of Sales Role and
then followed up with State Manager position. As the Senior
Sales Executive at Land Rover, I felt my role was pretty good,

but State level management definitely pricked my interest. All the same I was very loyal to my brand and tried to walk away. Then the two owners asked me to do one thing, and they promised that after that they would leave me be. They wanted me to meet their General Manager. They seemed convinced that once I'd met with him the role would be more attractive to me. My regular day off was Tuesday and so I agreed to meet with him for breakfast. What harm could it do? And hey, who doesn't enjoy being head hunted?

We arranged the breakfast meeting at Grey & Bliss café in Port Melbourne, not far from the head office of their business. With my brain always on the go, and the kids being at school on Tuesdays, I was interested to see what they felt I could bring to table, and what their business model was, salary and position were secondary to me at that point, as I felt almost 100% sure I wouldn't be taking the job anyway. I had always considered every job interview *practice*, and so planned to take the meeting and head into the city shopping for new work outfits afterwards.

The café was bustling with customers and the unmistakable smell of cooked breakfasts and hot coffees. It was a beautiful Melbourne day with the Sun already beating down heat onto the footpath as shoppers hurried by to the tune of reggae music from a busker seated not far from the doorway. I had underestimated how good it would feel to take job interviews whilst already in a great role, and found I was more relaxed than ever before. Perhaps that was the key I thought, to take meetings when you didn't really need to instead of waiting until you had to stress about it. I mused on whether or not I should have been thinking that way whilst filming for *Neighbours!* Perhaps I should have taken a leaf out of their book and started talks with *Home & Away? Sarah in Summer Bay?*

I rounded the corner of the café and sighted one of the business owners standing and waving his arms around wildly to get my attention, quite a wise move, as I am officially as blind as a bat. Beneath him sat a man with his head down writing notes on a pad and despite the aerial antics of his boss neglected to look in my direction even when I arrived tableside. It seemed rude and after greeting the owner with a handshake I waited to sit down until eye contact had been made between myself and the man I could only assume was the General Manager they had been desperate for me to meet. Eventually after a few uncomfortable moments of waiting for him to finish writing he looked up at me and immediately broke out into a cute sideways smile. Suddenly and cripplingly, I found it hard to breathe or speak. I had been struck dumb by the strongest force of attraction I had felt in my entire life and it took actual effort to continue on professionally. Within split seconds I was having internal dialogues to snap myself out of it, and after fumbling to pull out the chair managed to sit down and face him. I knew the business owner was talking because I could see in my peripheral vision that his mouth was moving, but I didn't hear a word he said. My eyes were locked tightly on those of the gorgeous creature sitting opposite me, and I was drowning in them. In those milliseconds I think I lived a lifetime, a lifetime of love, a lifetime of rapid decision making and a lifetime of searching and suddenly finding *The One*. I knew in that cataclysmic moment I wanted to give him everything, my money, my life, my body, me, and the realness of those feelings were as sure as you're holding Nicola Charles

Autobiography in your hands now. I had never believed it until that moment, never knew that it was possible, to meet someone and instantly *know,* and from where I was sitting, I was pretty sure the strength of it was being felt on both sides. I wanted to eat this man alive, drink him in and never let him go. But oh yeah, this was a job interview, oops.

His name was Nick, a Greek Australian with amber eyes and big lips. Was he good at his job? I'm sure he was, I really didn't care from that point on. Things I did note were muscular thighs bulging through his pants, tanned skin, gorgeous forearms and hands, and Oh, an unfortunate Wedding ring. Bugger. Sarah's affair came flooding back to me as I pulled on the brakes of my almost uncontrollable lust. Oh well, I guess taking the job was as irrelevant now as when I walked in because there was no way on earth I could accept working alongside someone I was this attracted to. No, no, no, no, no, no, no.

However, during the meeting Nick had to go to the bathroom, twice. Yes, twice he wafted past me leaving a hint of aftershave and *man* that left me weeping on the inside and

303

questioning why the Universe would choose to tease me so painfully, and on a Tuesday as well.

Twenty odd years I'd been living and working in Australia off and on and never had I been attracted to a Greek man. Twenty years earlier I had been living in Athens as a model with Elite for many months a year, and never had I been attracted to a Greek man, and yet here I was, going quietly bonkers to the point of almost fainting publicly over the General Manager of a fleet car company. Whoa, one never knows what's around the corner. But in all seriousness, underneath the inescapable clouds of sexual attraction that bristled between us like a constant energy source was a deep knowing that I found hard to explain. I was born in Worcestershire, England, over 17,000 kilometers away. He was born in South Yarra, Melbourne, to a conservative Greek family, and yet, it was as if we had been separated at birth. Made of the same materials, but somehow divided, his half sent in one direction, mine in the other.

"According to Greek mythology, humans were originally created with four arms, four legs and a head with two faces. Fearing their power, Zeus split them into two separate parts,

condemning them to spend their lives in search of their other halves."

Had we found our other halves? It certainly felt like it.

13

In an ongoing effort to be a good human being I had turned
down the job offer from the fleet car company for two reasons.
One, I had a perfectly good job working for an iconic British
car manufacturer, now owned by *Tata,* and two, I had a
bloodthirsty attraction to a potential new boss, and that simply
would not do. Cue round of applause for a rather stella effort
on my part! You're welcome!

Then, as I sat at my desk doing yet another online course that
would tutor me on the latest Range Rover designs an email
came in. It was from the General Manager of the fleet car
company, Nick. He asked if I would attend a dinner meeting
with them one last time at the Lobster Cave in Beaumaris later
that week, as they had a proposal that may be tough to turn
down. Did a touch of selfishness creep in when I read it?
Certainly. Would it require me to throw my rulebook on life
out of the window to attend? Yes. Did I accept? Of course I
did. Because somehow this *Twin Flame* of mine had chosen

my favorite food and restaurant without ever needing to ask me, and I can never turn down a good Lobster.

Clearly I had two reasons to be nervous as I drove into the car park adjacent to the restaurant that evening. The most exciting thing that had ever happened to me emotionally and sexually was fueling my decision making, and blind curiosity about the professional role had left me questioning everything, including how long I could go on spending one day a weekend away from my kids by remaining at the Dealership. Please always be nice to Dealership sales staff on Saturdays, they've given up part of their weekend to sell you a car.

I was both cursing the day these business owners had walked up to my desk at Land Rover and marveling at the sliding doors moments that could have prevented it ever happening. Because I had been scheduled to leave early that night, but had got caught up with a customer and so was there at 6.05pm when they approached my desk.

As I entered the restaurant a little early, I quickly headed to the bathroom ahead of the meeting, but as I navigated the tiny corridor at the back, I crashed straight into Nick who was leaving the gents at the same time. It was a devastatingly awkward moment, but as became our hallmark, the hand of *something* was now constantly pushing us together. I wanted to grab him and just stare into his eyes, no words needed, no explanation required, but once again I hit the brakes and made my apologies as I dove into the sanctuary of the loo to steady myself and catch my breath.

Once at the table Nick sat diagonally away from me, and studied me as I ordered the most expensive Lobster on the menu. I wanted to see how committed the business owners were and so pushed as many buttons as possible. Nick watched on as I ordered wine and chatted with the waiter, all the while observing every gesture of my hands giving no care to the fact that his fascination was clear for all to see. We were connected across the table by an invisible field of energy that kept drawing he and I ever closer together and a feeling of inevitability began to engulf us both. How close the Universe had come twice before to organizing this, and this was third time lucky. In 1993 we had both been on the Greek Islands at the same time, had we met, we would no doubt have six kids by now, maybe more. I was shooting for British catalogues and he travelling the country of his parents' birth in search of his heritage. In 1996 we were both planning to be at the 21st Century nightclub in Frankston, he with friends, and I on a booked Personal Appearance to sign autographs for Neighbours fans, but he changed plans last minute and headed into the city. However, this was 2017, and this time the Universe was clearly taking no prisoners.

I do remember hearing some of the things the business owners said before I decided to play like it was roulette, after all, I had nothing to lose, or did I? So as I gave Nick my strongest poker face I said *National Sales & Marketing Manager* or I'm out. The air hung heavy with the weight of the comment for quite a few moments before Nick said *I'm good with that.* One of the partners wished to consider it outside whilst smoking a cigarette and asked me if I'd like to join him.

Once outside the partner asked me *have you and Nick met before? No,* I replied, *never. I think you two will work well together,* he added. Was I really doing this? Was I leaving Land Rover and my dream job to work for what was essentially a start-up business? That would depend on what was said when I walked back inside.

Once we were all seated the partner who I had accompanied outside said *welcome aboard,* as Nick and I locked eyes knowing that we'd be spending an awful lot of time in each others company from that point on. What mattered most was that as the main bread winner for my kids I had moved one rung up the corporate ladder with the possibility of investigating what it was that hung in the air between this man and I.

Around this time my interest in Politics was becoming stratospheric. I had been asked two years prior to become part of Donald Trumps *Super PAC* and had gladly jumped on board to help in any way I could via my social media. Why? Because Trump had become an American Icon, a success at seemingly most things he had turned his hand to. He was blisteringly honest, sometimes too honest, very similar to myself, and about as far removed from a Politician as it was possible to get. He had led the life of a bona fide American playboy and had absolutely no *need* to run for office, only a *want* to, and for my money that would be an interesting experiment for a country steeped in corruption and party politics. All the same, it was still just a hobby and I wasn't living there anymore, but I knew one thing to be true, if America sneezed, the World caught a cold. I wanted the USA to move in a positive direction that worked for all citizens, not just the elites, and two of my children held American passports. I wanted there to be an America left for them when they grew up.

During that time, I was also asked to fill in on a little Sunday morning radio show. The regular female host was taking a short break and I was recommended to fill in. I had done short stints in radio off and on and had always felt very confident with it as a medium. Perhaps it was the studios and microphones feeling like a second home after all those years of voice-overs, but whatever it was, I felt like I could be myself *on-air*. Mostly because being an actor is so very different from being a radio personality. Being an actor is creating something beautiful while dragging along a ball and chain belonging to the writers and directors. It's their vision, their dialogue, their character and their ideas. The actor is just the living, breathing, vessel that delivers their vision, not only that, a *character* like *Sarah Beaumont* could be written out at whim, and was. On radio it was Nicola Charles, on radio the words were mine and on radio I felt free to create conversation organically.

What had begun as a pretty standard fill-in role rapidly became a lot more, as the two weeks on the radio show expanded to four. Following conversations with the shows creator Pete I was asked to contribute ideas and segments, seeing me become a Content Producer as well as Co-host. This struck chords in parts of me I didn't know existed. I was able to combine my British yearning for comedy with subject matter that wouldn't ordinarily warrant it. I found it cleverly allowed me to say quite insightful things about situations happening globally by making it satire. Unable to have listeners call in I thought it might be fun to mock up callers and have them be quite rude. What could be more fun I asked myself? Then it came to me. What could be *a lot* more fun would be if those rude calls were coming in from say *The Queen of England,* and let's make her *drunk* and yelling at Philip to pull his pyjama's up. I think it's fair to say that running outside the studio with my mobile phone and calling my own radio show to complain about the footie scores or politicians, whilst mimicking my own Queen *drunk* was just about as much fun as it's possible to have with your clothes on, and the funnier and harder it got to keep it all straight while live on air the more hilarious the segments became. Now of course with the passing of Prince Philip those clips will have an extra special place in my history. I eventually expanded the callers to Doris, the cockney singleton newly moved to Melbourne who couldn't get a date and Shazza the rather rough sounding Collingwood supporter with a crush on Jordan De Goey. Doing our little Sunday morning radio show became an absolute addiction and the cherry on top was knowing that my gorgeous Greek boss, who was now closely monitoring my every move in and out of work, would be listening in while walking his dog. It often felt as if I were doing the show just for him, to impress him, to make him laugh and to connect somehow across the great distance between us every Sunday morning. With my phone on silent I would often get text messages from him that would simply read *That was very funny,* and my colleagues would question, without really knowing who they were talking about, *Is he listening?* Those text messages were the most important human connection I'd had in years.

In the early days of my new role as the National Sales and Marketing Manager I would often spend almost all of my time on the road, visiting with existing partners and seeking out new ones. There is something extremely motivating about being given enough trust to work at that level and I knew that not only did I wish to succeed for the business I also wanted to do it for myself. I was once again visiting those remote panel shops and repair businesses that had been so welcoming to me just a couple of years earlier and they welcomed me back again with open arms. What was different however was that my new role required me to have weekly and sometimes daily face to face catch-ups with my General Manager, Nick. I knew I couldn't let him down, couldn't let the decision to hire me be a mistake, and so I made sure that whenever I was asked what's new, I had something to offer up. I literally worked like a demon.

Our catch-ups could not occur in the office environment. Young secretaries had already noticed the chemistry between us and were making comments, and so we took our meetings out for coffee around the corner from the office and needless to say they were quite long. Not once did either of us say or do anything inappropriate, beyond getting to know one another and having perhaps one too many coffees or hot chocolates before we said goodbye. Those meetings had become our touchstone, and both of us had quietly decided that knowing this, and admiring each other from afar was probably all we were ever going to get. I remember I removed my Wedding ring when I knew, quietly and without theatrics. I had only kept it there to deter unwanted advances from men at work, who were always careful to check if I had one, but now it felt obscene to keep wearing it when my heart was already owned. I had ended my marriage years earlier, though we remained under the same roof, and yet now I knew I needed a clean break. This man who was rapidly becoming my best friend and mentor, was always there for me, every step of the way. He never mentioned my ex-husbands name once, not even when I did, he just stood silently by my side as I made all the decisions for myself. I began to call him 007 as his personality was one of calm self-confidence, and of someone who carried many secrets, secrets that may take a lifetime to come out. He wasn't like any other man I had ever met, and I was becoming more magnetically drawn to him with every passing day, and would often say out loud as we walked towards each other *Magnets.*

Then, at a post-production breakfast one Sunday morning the radio-show asked if I would like the Co-host position permanently. I was flabbergasted, as it was totally unexpected, but gratefully accepted the offer and felt very excited to be part of something that felt like such a good fit. The show was called *That Radio Show!*

(PHOTO: That Radio Show! and radio in general has been quite simply my favorite job to date. The family you create is smaller and feels more intimate than the large family you need to create on a television or movie set. I'm more comfortable in smaller groups. Not agreeing was fine, as long as everybody got their say and we definitely did. They were my

words, not a writers and my actions to stand by, not a
Directors. I felt protective of these two men Pete and Eddie
and still do today, even though, just like a family, we get
ticked off with each other occasionally, mostly over politics.)

(PHOTO: Interacting and listening to guests was one of my
favorite things on the show. How can you know what another
person thinks about anything unless you ask them? Radio
makes us listen in ways television and film cannot. It is a
treasured medium as far as I am concerned. I miss it.)

With Peter Armstrong as host, myself as Co-host and Eddie
Olek on panel (technical stuff) who would also chime in. The
three of us often came from very different viewpoints on
things, which I loved. Often with co-hosts I've noticed a
tendency to try and agree when discussing topics and though
that works too, I prefer to hear differing viewpoints. This was
because I had become extremely anti viewpoint
discrimination. It was happening everywhere politically. The
Left attempting to shut down, dismiss and vilify the opinions
and beliefs of those on the right or center-right like myself,
and the political arena felt on the cusp of something worrying.
And so, as hoped, I began to use the platform to gradually
bring some politics into the discussion. We tackled the news
of the day, but with a twist. It was Sunday morning after all,
and nobody expected it to sound like news hour radio. The
listeners wanted real opinions, and the fact that they were
getting them from the actor who played Sarah Beaumont on
Neighbours made it all the more surprising for them. Before
long the fan mail and comments on my social media began
blowing up, as listeners from the UK started tuning in via the
SEN App and also tuning in to the You Tube clips I was
posting showing key moments from the show. Though they

very much loved the comedy we were bringing to segments they were also reacting extremely well to the conversations and opinions about politics. We began arranging appearances with celebrities and writers who had heard the show and wanted to come in, when out of the blue I got an email from Alan Fletcher. He was about to begin a tour of the UK in a show that would star both him and his wife. He asked me if they could use clips of Karl and Sarah for the show, and without hesitation I was happy to say yes, with a request that he would come and promote the show to our British listeners on That Radio Show! He agreed.

At that point I was determined to somehow take the show Monday to Friday, and also develop our growing global listenership, and so I was keen to use any and all contacts I had to get us there. Actors and Comedians in the UK all began talks with our little show in Melbourne, Australia to come in and co-host our show when they were in town for events like the Melbourne Comedy Festival, and it felt like we were moving in a very positive direction.

At work, things were changing within our business. As I had been warned years earlier the insurance companies were pulling rank on the Accident Replacement Vehicle industries seeing profits and recoveries taking a sharp downturn. Then, during a coffee meeting with my best friend and boss Nick he delivered some devastating news. After a year of working closely together he was leaving and moving into an entirely different profession. It was as if the World briefly stopped turning. How would I survive not seeing him almost daily? How could I be a radio host without knowing he'd be listening? How would my soul survive without him quietly guiding and supporting me? As he painfully told me,

You'll be okay.

And even as he said it, I knew he was trying to convince himself of the same as he displayed one of the best fake-bravery faces I'd ever seen.

Yeah, Yeah, I'll be fine.

His eyes darted around mine, searching for a reaction that might convey more than acceptance. So I called on all my acting skills to allow him to do this unencumbered by any feelings I might have about it, and let him go, doing what I always do and making it easier for the other person, though the very real pain in my heart was grinding my limbs to a static halt, as if my bloodstream had become instantaneously filled with lead.

We returned to the office to close out what we needed to, as secretaries and assistants alike slowly became dumbfounded that he'd be leaving us, and I could see his shoulders slowly deflate as we crept ever closer to the final goodbye.

That took place outside in the car park, with no doubt the entire office looking on through the first-floor windows, but we would never have known, we were just locked in the horror of what was happening. I kept things straight, professional and proper, until the moment we knew we had to hug goodbye. We had been working together by then for around twelve months, and we had never touched one another, not once. And so I grabbed him as a friend, hugged him farewell and waited for the release that would see the end of Nick & Nic the team that had quadrupled the businesses revenue, except he didn't let go, not for quite some time. Eventually I fell closer to him, afraid to let myself become teased by what might have been, as the hug went on.

I did find the strength to pull back and walk away eventually, and as I did, I felt once again proud that the girl from Worcestershire who very much needed him, had done the right thing. I didn't know what he was thinking as he drove off, how could I? But I guessed it wasn't anything good, because he seemed to find it hard to breathe as he walked away.

14

I decided to resign from the business soon afterwards and have a crack at running my own. I had all the contacts and experience and so would try my hand at brokering fleet hire. I really didn't have a choice in the matter, Nick and I had become a corporate team, we had made strategic plans together to grow the business and the important relationships to it, and I didn't relish the thought of explaining to everyone that Nick had moved on, which I knew would affect their confidence in us. I remember one partner I had a close relationship with, a woman a little older than myself who'd had boardrooms with Nick and I over the years, asking me where he was. I felt comfortable enough to tell her the truth of what was happening which caused her to ask pointedly,

So, will you be seeing him again?

No? I replied. *We said goodbye. He's left the industry.*

GOD YOU'RE A FUCKING IDIOT! She exclaimed.

Shocked at the sudden change of tone I was snapped out of business mode and into a personal conversation.

Why's that? I asked.

Because he's clearly in fucking love with you! She continued.

I could barely speak or move. She had said out loud the thing I had been grappling with for over a year and as she did, I began to panic. I hadn't imagined that it was plain for others to see, and that single moment with a business partner polarized everything, but he was gone, and I had absolutely no way to contact him.

I soldiered on with the radio show as my co-hosts watched me briefly fall apart convincing myself that I had become less funny on-air and that Nick was no longer listening. Friends said helpful things like *Plenty more fish in the sea* and *I mean come on, you're Sarah Beaumont, he's out there!*
But I somehow knew it would be Nick until the end of time even though I had absolutely no way of ever contacting him again. I remember I googled him, just once, to check for a

LinkedIn account or something else that would keep him on the map, but there was very little, just a couple of mentions about Golf Tournaments he had placed in. His love of Golf was a side of his life he had never shared with me and I told myself there had been a reason why, and that reason was that the whole connection had been imagined somehow. It was easier that way anyway, to tell myself it was wishful thinking on my part, as I scrambled to protect my heart from the pain. I do that a lot in life, having made some truly horrendous decisions over the years.

Then, twelve weeks later on a hot Melbourne morning as I headed out on the School run through our busy beach community the phone rang from a number I didn't recognize. I can remember exactly which traffic light I was waiting at when it happened and how I genuinely wasn't sure who it was at first. The voice said,

Hi it's Nick.

Nick who? I replied, having at least nine Nicks in my call list that would ordinarily have their numbers identified.

How flattering, the voice continued, *that's a good start!*

And there was Nick's sarcasm, right back in my car where it belonged.

More than anyone I had ever met he was the one who told it to me straight, hid nothing, wore who he was in bright neon on his sleeve and made it clear that he was there by choice and that choice was his to make. To say Nick is no nonsense would be a criminal understatement. It's why he is so successful in his chosen profession, or should I say professions, as he has moved his talents for business around a couple of industries, and why more than anyone else I'd worked alongside, knew his own value. Born in Australia to Greek parents under the astrological sign of Aries, Nick was the guy that wouldn't sugar coat a thing, so receiving an impromptu call from him, twelve weeks after a difficult goodbye, was big. It meant of course that he had spent the entire time considering this action, the pros and the cons, the outcomes and the tears, and made the call anyway. I had my answer. That being that what we had between us was valuable to him as well as me.

It was a step into the unknown to meet him for coffee without a valid work reason to. He touched on helping me set up my new business, but we both knew the real reason we were there. I felt in my bones that the thinly veiled blanket of a happy marriage he had been languishing behind was now gone, and so we spoke a lot of truth. The first thing that always strikes me about Nick when he walks into a room is his scent, as emotion meets a man that makes me want to bury my head in his body and live there til the end of time surrounded by the musk of his obvious desire. He makes me want to live inside his clothes and camp out there all day so that I can drift off on an ocean of sex and maleness. Nothing and no-one compared to the feeling of his embrace as merely breathing him in sent me into a state of delirium and I would often physically sway requiring him to catch me and snap me out of it. He is one incredibly sexy man.

I finally escaped the clutches of his passionate hug hello and sat to face him at a small table in a cosy café in Moorabbin. The café owner walked past us three or four times as our eyes locked, deciding not to break our gaze just yet, before eventually appearing at our sides to say,

My God we can feel the energy from you two from over there!

It wasn't the first or the last time we'd have that kind of comment said to us, and after ordering a drink he took the menu out of my hands to pass it back to her and as he did his fingers brushed onto mine. My entire body blew up with a fire that felt like tiny pin pricks from head to toe. The madness of the attraction was inescapable and yet still we had done nothing about it. We hadn't kissed, we hadn't made love, we had only hugged, and yet... we knew.

It had been a year at this point, a year of what had essentially become foreplay, and the ongoing agony and ecstasy of it was both pleasure and pain. I played along for what must have been weeks, him never pushing me one way or the other, never clarifying what this was, only basking in it, for it was glorious, for as long as the Universe allowed it to exist. Our conversations were abstract, and sometimes I would say to him,

Whatever you do, please don't break it.

He would always reply, *I won't. Not ever.*

Then about eight weeks after our reconnection I remember turning my car off the Hume Freeway at Sydney Road near Coburg (not a particularly glamorous part of town and very industrial) and feeling woefully unwell. Convincing myself I was having a heart attack I flew through the lights and down a side road before pulling onto a grassy nature strip and falling out of my door onto the grass gasping for air. I can't know how long I was there on the ground trying desperately to breathe because everything had become a blur. As I lay panting in the uncut grass a car stopped to enquire if I was okay, naturally assuming I'd had some kind of traffic collision. I made it back onto my seat and looked up at the blistering blue Australian sky wondering if it would be the last thing I ever saw, and how ironic that would be after years of struggle to make it back there. The heat of the air was comforting and I was engulfed with a feeling I will never forget before suddenly throwing up next to the car.

I had fallen crazy in love with Nick, my married boss. I had found *the one*. It wasn't just the intense sexual attraction between us, it was who he was, what he stood for and how his soul was built. It was the fact he was going to sacrifice us and never expect this connection to become anything. It was his undying loyalty and friendship and the fact that he was more of a supportive partner in my life than any man I had ever known.

And now life was going to get very tricky indeed.

I waited maybe twenty minutes before attempting to drive, cancelled my meeting and headed home, all the while deciding whether or not I should tell him and put into words the unspoken thing we already knew. I was 48 years old at the time and I never expected to feel this way about anyone at this time in my life. Something about middle age makes you appreciate the people that matter most and spring clean those who are not healthy for you, and as I was pondering that thought a truck suddenly cut me off as I merged onto the Freeway, almost clipping my car and causing me to swerve to avoid a collision. I asked myself,

What if something happened to either one of us and he didn't know? Didn't know that I deeply loved him?

I decided that couldn't happen. True, we may never be together, just might not be possible, but wherever life took Nick, I wanted him to know he was loved by me. So when almost home I pulled over and dialed his personal number, the same one he'd reconnected with me on. I often think about the fragility of that connection, the sliding doors moment that if he hadn't called *me* from that number some weeks earlier, I would have had no idea how to find him again.

He picked up immediately, as he always did, not once since the day we met had he not picked up a call from me, even if he was in a meeting, he would message straight away that he'd call me back and always did. No-one had ever made me feel as relevant and important in their life as he did, and with every moment shared, even by phone, it was as if the Sun was coming up around me. But this time as I spoke it wasn't as his colleague or friend anymore, it was the person we all are deep down inside when we are raw and exposed and taking a leap of faith into the unknown, the bravery that had a faint whiff of what it had taken to run with an audition I hadn't been expecting with Jan Russ. The tone of my voice was clearly new and as yet unheard by him.

Hi it's me, I said.

Oooo this sounds serious, he replied.

I need to talk to you.

There was a brief moment, only slight, one that confirmed to me he could read me like no other even on the phone,

I'm assuming this is something we need to do in person? He asked.

Yes, I said, *yes, it is.*

We arranged to meet the following morning at a coffee shop near neither of our homes and away from businesses and customers that might recognize us, though that was always more tricky for me than him, still dragging that Soap Star ball and chain along next to me wherever I went.
It was a typically dreary hole of a café near Tullamarine Airport and as I parked my car facing it, I suddenly got what I can only describe as my first ever experience of stage fright. I

had appeared in over sixty television commercials Worldwide, attended personal appearances with thousands of screaming *Neighbours* fans, filmed the role of a femme fatale for an Australian Soap Opera watched in over fifty countries and walked the runway in fashion shows in London and Melbourne, and yet, this single moment became the most heart-stopping thing I had ever done, because life is a bit like that for all of us. It's easy today with social media to appear ballsy, or sexy, or confident, or pretty much anything you want to be. Filming with cameras and crew for an unknown audience was easy, but this wasn't social media, or filming, this was Nick, and I was becoming patently aware that what I was about to do could see me lose him, even as a friend, forever. I headed inside to find a table.

Strangely, I had decided to dress appallingly that day. Something odd and typically Nicola had occurred in my brain as an inner dialogue had told me to dress *down* for the *talk*. I guess I didn't want him to be swayed by a sexy outfit, or stylish appearance *not that I do style particularly well*. No, I wanted him to just hear me, the real me, and feel it.

So in grey tracksuit pants and an old sweater I found a table and sat down for what felt like my first coronary.

As Nick walked in and towards me my heart began beating out of my chest and my feet extended as if they were getting cramp. I was having a massively physical reaction to the stress. He too looked discombobulated and I began to experience feelings of guilt, after all, neither of us would ever be the same people again if I managed to say what I wanted to. I didn't stand and hug him this time, I simply said *Hi* as I looked up nervously at him.

His face betrayed a mixture of fear and apprehension as both of us began breathing heavily. The usual urge was there for both of us, to reach across and grab the other and never let go, but this was a public café on a busy Melbourne morning and so we used every ounce of self-control we had to simply sit and stare at each other. Then he spoke.

What's this all about?

It wasn't as naïve as it looks written down there, and so I opened my mouth to speak the single question that had been dancing around my brain for over a year, only nothing came out.

I tried again,

Tell me………..

Tell me………..

Tell me………..

He smiled the way he always does, a little sideways, showing his dimples and the kindness of his soul.

Come on, spit it out, you dragged me here. He pushed.

I tried with all my might to ask it. In fact, I tried for almost half an hour. During my attempts we'd found time to order coffees and drink them, as I continued to fumble and stumble around the simple task that lay ahead. Eventually I had a final internal dialogue and told myself that it was now or never.

"Tell me it doesn't exist?"

He looked deeply into my eyes in a way he had never allowed himself to before, devouring my soul as I felt like I was being eaten alive by a wolf, as he allowed the words that had clearly captivated him to hang in the air. The question had felt like jumping off a cliff and now I had to wait and see if he would catch me or I'd hit the bottom and smash into a million pieces. And then he said two words.

"I can't."

It's really something to have a thing like that confirmed, to know you are not mad, not alone, not deluded in some way. I've spent my entire life second-guessing myself, making bad choices, strange choices, choices I should have taken longer to consider and think about, like resigning from *Neighbours* when I should have stayed, like agreeing to go to Los Angeles when I had no business being there, and like telling no-one when a neighbour assaulted me as a child. I knew this time that a year of waiting was enough for anyone and the physical and emotional toll it was taking on us both had become too much. Nick had already told me he was walking for two hours every morning from 5am thinking about his life, and now my bold move had somewhat released the pressure for us both.

Then he repeated my question.

"Tell me it doesn't exist? No-one could say that but you. Your words are just, they're just beautiful."

We sat in his car and I told him that whatever happened next was his choice and that I simply needed him to know. I reached over and held his hand, which in itself was one of the most intimate moments of my life. Nick's hands are huge and this was the first time I had ever touched them outside of a handshake.

We didn't kiss and instead I walked away from him that day not knowing what would become of us, but as he glanced at me as I walked back to the Land Rover, I knew that whatever was coming, was going to be good.

15

And suddenly I had wings.

Somehow, I had reconnected with who I was when I was four years old, who I was before being thrown to the floor by an adult I trusted, who I should have been during my marriages, and who I could now become because the Love lifted me. The arrested development the abuse had caused had been punched through like a knife through butter. I didn't need to marry it to see if it would *work out,* I had no questions about Love left, I was just feeling it and it felt like a completed circle, whole again, or maybe just for the first time. It wasn't lonely like fame, with its *Feast or Famine,* there one minute and gone the next, it had depth, it was real, and more importantly, it was happening.

Like someone firing the starting pistol at a race our emotional love affair had begun and its power was a hurricane that I knew nothing and no-one would able to stop.

(PHOTO: Looking into Nick's eyes is like looking into a mirror. We knew so much about each other without words. One born in Worcestershire, England one in Melbourne, Australia and yet, it's as if we lived parallel lives. I want to take care of him for the rest of my life, feed him soup when he's old and give him everything I own. That was the key to Love. Knowing what you were prepared to give. I hadn't known until that moment.)

My on-air personality on radio had received a mighty injection
of vigor as the lyrics of my own song *Alive Again* played on
an endless loop in my head. No drug, no injection, no vitamin
or tonic could ever feel this good and give so much strength, I
felt invincible. But there was one small shard of pain that
splintered in my side as a daily reminder that our path would
not be a simple one, the splinter that reminded me that we
couldn't tell anyone. Nick needed to end his marriage, tend to
his affairs and be the descent human being he had always
been, and that situation was going to take time. I knew that no
matter the wait, the trials this would bring, I had no choice but
to ride it out. We have no choice with affairs of the heart, we
fall in love in the most unexpected places. Of the few friends
that did know of our love I received comments like,

OMG the press will say you're just like Sarah Beaumont!

You'll be labeled a home wrecker!

But only someone who truly knows who I am in the dark
corners of my being where my four-year old self lives would
know that I couldn't give a crap what others might say, never

did care, never would. You only have to look at my social media to understand that and now perhaps this book. I played the game of caring for far too long. Played *The Game* of being what was sought, instead of being myself. It was like a prison and for over thirty years I had wondered when the day would come that I might escape it. The escape had come through adversity, as it often does. It had come through filing customer records at Mercedes-Benz and experiencing the kind of ego death that occurs when a co-star from your TV show barely acknowledges your existence because you had fallen so far down life's ladder, and that even though the slip had occurred because you placed every resource you had into a court case to keep your children, it meant nothing to most people. It had come during one of my first coffee meetings with Nick when we first met and I heard myself answer a question he asked me,

What about your media career?

It's over. I said. *I'm a has-been.*

No you're not, he replied, *there's nothing has-been about you, you're a talented gun.*

And suddenly someone believing in you makes all the difference. How could I question the morality of pure Love? For the sheer fact that we had fallen so hard for each other displayed to me clearly that neither of us had ever felt this way about anyone else before, and we became singularly locked in on what we had found, a pot of gold waiting for us in the most unlikely of places, a fleet car hire company in Port Melbourne. My happiness was becoming increasingly apparent around the traps in Melbourne, and so of course, the haters arrived. It was during this time that I realized all that glitters is not gold, in fact many of the female acquaintances I had made socially, even those I had done favors for, were suddenly in the business of crapping all over my new found happiness. I began hearing second hand gossip about myself and eventually received a hefty and unwarranted slap in the face when I lost a friend due to the lie of a meddling woman who couldn't stand the thought of the friendship. I didn't wish to repair anything with any of them or engage in their schoolgirl bitchfests, I'd been there and done that as a model and on

Neighbours, and so instead I began writing my novel *The Witches of Toorak*. The more the hate and shade came from these women who had married for money and were now left languishing in their unhappy marriages, the more content I acquired for my book. It was a stroke of genius and saw me thank them for each and every new incident of their insecurity as I scribbled them down frantically in my notebook and on my phone. I had previously released *Click Monkey*, a crippling hard book to write as I chronicled the life of Ingrid, a woman indoctrinated into abuse as a child by her family who then unconsciously sought it out again as an adult. I wasn't sure I'd ever write anything again to be honest, but with this much material satelliting around me the opportunity was too good to pass up. As news of the book began to circulate, I started getting phone calls from journalists, who told me about their own experiences with the women of Toorak and the entire project just grew and grew. *The Witches of Toorak* it seemed was going to strike a chord, at least domestically, and so it became a great focus for me during the lonely months I waited for Nick, snatching only brief moments together to re-charge our Love batteries before parting again for him to manage his affairs.

343

It was around that time I began to notice all of my close relationships polarizing as slowly the gulf between those who were happy for me and those that were not began to widen. I am someone that is always selfishly grateful when my friends are happy and doing well in life because then I don't have to worry about them and can focus more on the friends that are not doing so well, but it seemed that attitude was not shared by all when it came to Nick and I. Labels began appearing when it came to me along with more second hand gossip that had originated from bored housewives and jealous socialites as the fondness for inglorious behaviors from Melbourne females became all too apparent. My *Neighbours* character was often rolled into the dialogue, as it was just too easy to equate my extra-marital affair with that of *Miss Sarah Beaumont*. I shouldn't have been surprised at the reach for such an easy comparison as they tried and succeeded in multiple attempts to slander me far and wide, and yet I was. Women can talk endlessly about supporting each other but in reality, they often enjoy tearing each other down a lot more. Righteous indignation is a powerful drug it seems. It's not a pleasant thing to admit to, being a woman myself, it is however an inescapable fact that women can be very nasty bitches, and so *The Witches of Toorak* rolled on, morning after morning from 3-6am, my preferred writing time, with the press already talking about a book that wasn't finished yet, as the Authors dream of having a book heavily anticipated began to unfold. I remember during that year a photographer, again someone I had done favors for, said a jaw dropping comment to me about my career. He said with a straight face,

I can make you or break you. I can bring you back baby.

The comment was a perfect example of the naivety and hubris of many in Melbourne. My career had spanned many disciplines and multiple decades. I had worked my arse off all on my own since I was eighteen years old. I had left my family behind and traveled the World as a slave to the camera, starving to death to fit the mold of *Top Model.* I had gone deep inside myself to create an iconic character in a long running TV show, was now a struggling first generation immigrant with three children and was writing my third book, and yet, this man had told himself he had the power to change my future or remove my past by simply making me look good in a photograph. I can't explain even to myself why this happens around fame but it always does, people enter your life, tell themselves they are going to be the most important connection you've ever made and then spend a lot of time believing that. If I know one thing about myself to be true it is that until 2017 I was a lone Wolf. Just like a Wolf, an attack at five years old had soured me somewhat to the joys of life and made me more weary and aggressive internally than I otherwise might have been. Just like a Wolf I trusted no-one and walked a lonely path around the World carving out basic survival for myself, and just like a Wolf it all looked very attractive from the outside as I dealt with massive amounts of inner turmoil. You don't walk up on a Wolf and start telling it what to do, not unless you're stupid, and clearly many of these people were. There's a very British saying about not suffering fools gladly and it was ringing very true in my ears as I navigated my new existence in Melbourne, not as a soap star, not even an actress, just a single working Mother of three.

(PHOTO: You don't walk up on a Wolf and tell it what to do.
You respect its history, its integrity and its strength. It's
something that frustrates me about human beings. We judge
on looks, looks, looks. I realize as a model I was part of that
problem, but somehow that gives me a unique perspective. We
must understand that we can never know another person's
pain, or what they have been through, and until we do,

347

assumptions about them are a dangerous thing. My dogs
don't make assumptions. Every day is a new day, and every
day they greet me as if for the first time and check-in. It's
respect, and dogs have it in abundance when compared to
most humans I've met.)

A childhood accident had left me with only 5% vision in my
right eye. I don't think I've ever told anybody that. Sight is
something I have struggled with my entire life. It may be why
the font is large in this book! I struggle badly with sight.
Unable to read or write without my glasses on I developed
from a very young age a different way *to see.* As this
happened when I was approximately four years old my ability
to develop other senses to compensate was greater and as a
result my sense of smell is off the charts. I can meet someone
new at a bar and whilst shaking their hand tell you exactly
which drugs they have taken and alcohol they have drunk. It
sounds crazy I know, but I can. But the sense I appreciate the
most is my ability to see through people. It has occasionally
let me down, but generally it's been extremely helpful. You
can smile and be friendly all your like, but if you wish me
malice, I can see it, I can smell it and I can taste it in the air.

That is why my children call me the *She Wolf* and I know I am not alone. Other people I have spoken to who lost particularly sight as a sense have had similar experiences.

Here's the thing my haters and detractors never understood about me. I will *never* apologize for who I am or change in order to fit inside their tiny little narrow-minded boxes, and I certainly won't become *like them.* I won't seek out a wealthy sponsor husband to please a model agent or socialite friends, I won't put money above Love and I won't spend my days worrying what other women are doing with their lives. But I will use their behaviors to fill pages of books and I thank them at least for that.

Every decision Nick made about us he made slowly and methodically, he simply refused to be rushed. What we were heading towards wasn't some quick bang somewhere to *get it out of our system.* No, for us it was a Love mountain we needed to climb, it was potentially the rest of our lives, and so we planned to spend the night away together in order to be alone. The day before leaving we felt we needed to catch up and always happy to be silently in each other's company we went to the movies in a country town far away. It was the middle of the day and it was only us and another couple sat on the other side of the theatre. I think it was one of those Deadpool movies, but I didn't hear a word that was said by any of the actors. I turned to Nick, reclined in his seat, and felt his breath gently touch my face. I had to kiss him, I needed to kiss him, I had waited over a year and tomorrow was a whole twenty-four hours away. I looked at his eyes as they flashed pure passion into mine and I said,

If we do this we will never be the same people again.

He said, *I know.*

The Kiss - REAL LIFE

This was no *Sarah Beaumont KISS.*

This was a desire like no other between two people crazy in Love and I fell into the warm soup of two souls feeling a mixture of core shaking arousal and of coming home. It was him, the fantasy lover of my dreams I had never forgotten about since I was a teenage girl. There was not one moment of gazing into each other's eyes, or pulling each other ever closer that didn't feel like fate coming to fruition. The intense relief of a lifelong search being *over* filled me with joy. I wondered if I'd feel embarrassed as I looked into his eyes having confirmed *a feeling,* but there was none, only two people who now had someone to Love.

We left that movie theatre with our hands clasped tightly together and shaking like leaves as our bodies began a twenty-four-hour anticipation marathon ahead of our journey to spend our first night away together.

The car ride there was torture, as I watched the side of his face as he drove us into deep countryside. I still had so many questions about him, and yet somehow I knew the time for talking was over, for now.

There are few things in life that can be predicted ahead of time and yet we can be doing something fairly innocuous and find our lives colliding with someone who is at that moment a stranger, and yet feel you have known them your entire life, maybe even multiple lifetimes. Feel that you have the possibility of a big future with them, and yet how could you know that? That single experience with Nick made me question everything, made me realize that there are things we can both know and not know all at the same time. Meeting Nick felt like a celestial reward for all the horrible things I had seen and been exposed to in life, a prize for walking through the heavy mud of life alone and making it to the other side, where the fields were green and the sun was shining. So I did something for the first time in my life, I stopped looking back, and I started looking *forward.* That was the gift Nick's Love gave me, a future.

(PHOTO: Our Love was attaching a new label to two people who didn't deserve it, that being that we were now having an

affair. It wasn't who we were and so we faced the knowledge
that the next year "at least" was going to be hell.)

We arrived at a secret location far from the city in the hopes
that no-one knew us there. The owners were Japanese artists
who had set up a beautiful guest getaway alongside their home
and neither spoke particularly good English or had any idea
who we were, it was perfect. When we got inside the blue
wooden cabin, we lit the fire as it was a chilly night and
waited for the owner who was busying herself with
instructions on how to do this and that, to leave. Nick closed
the door behind her and walked immediately towards me with
such purpose I felt a little afraid and hunted. I was standing up
on the fireplace warming the back of my legs and he bent
down and buried his head in my stomach and wrapped his
arms tightly around me. This is what we had waited for. This
was everything we had ever wanted. Peace, quiet and time
alone. Oh how we had craved just time alone.

I became a grown up in that room alone with Nick, and so
much more. I allowed myself to be *Nic,* not *Nicola Charles* or
any of the various other incarnations my life of pretending had

required me to be. I trusted him, and him I, and so I allowed this man who I was now desperately in love with, to get to know the real me. A country girl in leggings and wellington boots, messy hair and very little make-up. I had reached that point in my life where I no longer wanted to hide or pretend. Pretending was for fools, it wasn't living and it wasn't real like this. I wanted honesty, and freedom and only genuine Love around me.

It seemed as time went on that the less I tried to impress and the more I just allowed myself to *be* the harder we fell into each other, him amazed that I was nothing like my public self, and I relieved the façade was over. My defensive walls were down and we began talking about our greatest fears, our biggest dreams, including those that had never come to fruition, and all the while I sensed a bucket of secrets inside him he was not yet ready to tell me about. He had clearly been starved of love and peace and in an emotional space where he wasn't even sure he *deserved* happiness. He seemed broken down and trampled on, like the last survivor of an interplanetary prison camp that had been picked up whilst drifting in outer space by my lifeboat. I realized there was going to be a lot to discover, but I had absolutely no idea how unexpected the truth would be.

The Witches of Toorak was released by my baby publishing company to an excited audience of readers and reviewers, with one of the best litmus tests being the conversations had by a book store owner in Toorak itself. Purchasing more copies than any other store location in Australia I began marveling at the volume she was shifting. She told me that she had previously had a book for sale about dog walking but because it had the word Toorak on the cover the locals lapped it up, if you'll pardon the pun. She explained that the women of *Toorak* itself couldn't get enough of the book, mostly because they were concerned about their brothers and sons falling foul of these types of women. Suddenly the conversations I was having in Melbourne took a drastic turn with multiple females in journalism, media and society telling me they too had experienced the kind of people chronicled in the book. I had long phone chats with women who had since moved overseas who could still not forget their own encounters with the women of Toorak. In all honesty the suburb wasn't singled out particularly for having the largest density of bitches, sorry witches, merely that the quality and voracity of their character seemed more polarized there somehow. As most had married for their money they lived in constant fear of losing it all and so went on the attack with any potential threat that dare enter their circles, actively gleaming joy from smearing the names and reputations of those females who specifically had made their own money and built their own careers. It all seems ridiculous now with what the World has had to face in the aftermath but I have absolutely no doubt that their hate will follow them to their graves, Worldwide Pandemics not withstanding.

And so the release did something unexpected. It adjusted my Crown; it adjusted my ball and chain. I was no longer *only* Sarah Beaumont, or Nicola Charles from *Neighbours,* I was also *Author Nicola Charles*. I knew it must be true, because Wikipedia said so.

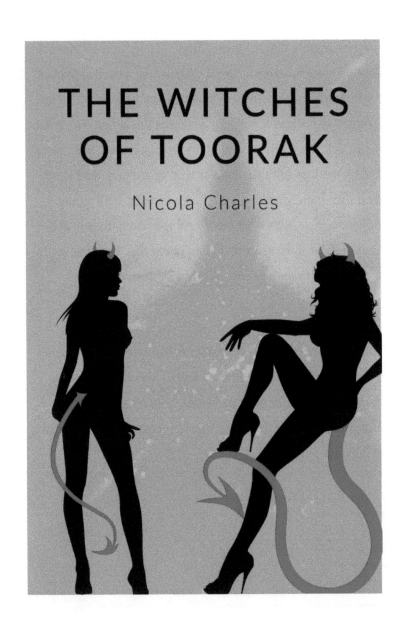

THE WITCHES OF TOORAK

Nicola Charles

(PHOTO: The Witches of Toorak did more than just expose the malevolent behaviors of women seeking career marriages in Melbourne, it also changed my Bio, from Neighbours star to "Author")

17

I was on board!

And my runaway Love train was leaving the station!

Nick left his marriage and we began our life together!

It was miraculous! Mind-blowing! Life affirming!

Nothing and no-one could stop this Love! No-sir-eee!!!!

But within a period of about eight weeks at the beginning of 2020 four huge freight trains collided in a perfect storm of destruction and threatened to end it all, one way or another.

Freight train one.

A once in a century Pandemic took down our World.

Freight train two.

I fell ill with Covid-19 and believed I was dying.

Freight train three.

I lost my beloved radio show that had given me purpose, a voice and the foundation for a radio career.

Freight train four.

I discovered Nick's secret and it shook me to my spiritual core.

And so like so many others on this beautiful planet of ours my World shifted....

....and if you thought I was political on radio prior to 2020, you hadn't seen anything yet.

The language around the Pandemic in early March 2020 seemed too unbelievable to be true. How can our World leaders have allowed this to happen? Whether it originated from Bats or a Lab surely this was incompetence on a Global scale? And if it wasn't incompetence, but something more sinister, why were we not allowed to investigate that without being cancelled? But despite believing in what I considered to be quite a voracious press I started witnessing what felt like a meteoric shift in the narrative. It made me very afraid indeed because as a Brit the free press had been something I had taken for granted. Something I assumed would always be there, a constant whistleblower if you like, as a very public checks and balances sheet. Instead, we had what gave most of us *chills*. They were attempting to *normalize* this, either to prevent panic or to create so much disinformation we would likely never know the truth as it became ever more buried in scandals, rumors and political correctness. I was pissed off.

Suddenly my particular type of voice was frowned upon, as telling *my own truth* was something that was no longer *allowed*. No longer *allowed?* I thought. Allowed by *who*? Don't we live in a free country?

"Isms" and the use of the English language to demonize anyone attempting to think for themselves or drudge through the mire of information were starting to be weaponized. While the elites in both politics and industry fought hard to achieve group think, the majority of people that followed my social media platforms were as perplexed as I was. I felt a marching loyalty to my fans and made the decision to share information I was getting with them. An *End of the World* type feeling began overtaking me and I made a conscious decision that if I was going down, I was going down in a blaze of honesty, and

361

so at a crucial time, and whilst still on *That Radio Show!* I publicly spoke out, as producers and technicians looked on in fear of what I might say next through the glass walls of the studio. I did my research, I found my own facts, and I spoke to them. No more, no less.

Then, as I entered the studio one Sunday morning in late March, I felt a painful scratching in the back of my throat and a headache like the worst hangover I'd ever had times twenty. I remember joking with Eddie about maybe having Corona and him spraying me with Glen20 as I sat in my seat. We could never have known the truth of what was coming, and I even posted a funny social media photo to push the show holding the can of disinfectant he had sprayed me with. Two weeks later I wasn't getting better and Pete took the decision to end the show at that time, which was only about a week before the entire studio shut down anyway. I was beyond devastated. The show was more than just a radio show for us of all. We had been reasonably unedited throughout our run, were quite controversial and had a listenership that spanned multiple continents, as fans listened in via the App. It caused me to hit a low for sure, as we all do when we lose our dream job, and that had a remarkable effect on the flu I could seemingly not shift.

It went from flu to hell in a matter of hours.

I remember sitting on my couch and saying through a blurred haze to my teenage daughter,

Something is inside me.

She replied, *Geez Mum that's dramatic.*

I have been called a liar so many times for sharing my experience of Covid-19 I've lost count. What's strange is that the people trying to invalidate me and my experience and who are accusing me of scaremongering are the very same people who are screaming at others on their own social media platforms about making sure they wear their mask. It's a prime example of the blatant hypocrisy that goes on in the minds of the far-left. They seek to invalidate *anything* that those who don't agree with them say, even when it *does* actually agree with them. I also noted clear activity on my accounts by what appeared to be *bots* who had isolated my media as belonging to a dissenter, and so began the pre-set algorithms to answer any reference with a typically insulting retort, usually something like *OMG take a look at yourself.* The comments were so common and so similar it was clearly not originating from a human, and were originating from accounts with no followers, and had been designed by Psychologists to attempt to damage the confidence of the author of the post. Luckily my skin is thick, but I have many friends and contacts driven off social media with this clever, but reasonably transparent tactic in 2020.

I made a decision, which I knew would likely cost me my acting career, to continue to try and get the truth out there. At that point the scaremongering that had already occurred on traditional media had worked a treat, even on me, because after weeks of saying to myself *No no this can't be Covid,* I now believed I was going to die. I wrote my Will, planned my funeral with Nick and as advised by the government hotline, said a meaningful goodbye to my kids. However, they also advised me to dial 000 and go to hospital, and that is something I decided not to do. I'm old-fashioned like that still believing that we have a choice where to die, although how long we have that is anyone's guess. It does sound morbid I know, but I guess morbid is something we all had to face in 2020.

I am the kind of person that rarely even takes a tablet for a headache. I battle through hangovers and work through colds and flu. I left hospital on the day I gave birth with all three children despite stitches and other issues and generally believed myself to be super-fit for my age. I remember at age forty-five having one of those medical tests that determines genetic age, and it coming back saying I was thirty-six years old, based on blood tests and fitness level. I was running around twenty-seven kilometers a week and had thighs so tight I could crack a walnut between them, and yet, this thing had taken me down so far that even as an Atheist I was praying to God to save me!

Luckily my friend Sally had posted me one of her asthma inhalers *just in case* I reached the point of not being able to breathe. She did this following a phone call where she could hear the breathing distress I was in. I am in absolutely no doubt that thing saved my life on two very bad days, so thank you so much Sally.

But what surprised me as a freedom loving, truth seeking whistleblower is that I also loved locking down. I almost dislike myself for saying that because having our liberty removed from us is something that on paper I am against, but the reality of it worked for me. It forced families to be together and one thing I knew for sure was that it would make or break my relationship with Nick, and I am relieved to say it made it.

What 2020 seemed to do for us was condense what would have been maybe two to three years of a relationship into one year. It also gave us quality time to talk.

I discovered something about him that explained an awful lot. It explained why he seemed to believe he didn't *deserve* to be happy, why he seemed broken down and often seemed *afraid*. Without divulging too much about another person's life I know that through his Christian beliefs he had been meticulously controlled and manipulated both financially and emotionally. It was very much the frog in boiling water scenario, as in it happened over time and crept up on him, everything was planned, from the purchase of furniture to whether or not he could own a car, and the timing of those purchases were given deadlines. They told him what he could and could not tell his parents, that was crucial, because they knew his parents would pull him away from it. They would often comment that if he faltered from what they called *The Path* there would be *Consequences*. *"Consequences"* was a word they used a lot and they made him wear a wristband so that he wouldn't forget it. They successfully used the fear of God to manipulate an innocent man until he bowed to their crushing will. I remember I cried when he told me, demanded he remove the wristband, which he did, and tear himself away from people who were clearly lying about wishing to help him and just enjoying the control side of things, particularly financially. He was a man who worked two jobs six days a week, removing time he desperately wanted to spend with his Son to satisfy their demands. The delusions these people told themselves and pulled others into were quite extreme, so much so that the worst parts of their story can't even be shared here, but I will definitely pen them into a horror story somewhere down the track.

And so my beautiful man and I spent 2020 talking endlessly and undoing as much of the damage as we could. It made the year count, it made it a very important one, and it made the sacrifices we were all making worth it.

I came a long way around the World from Worcestershire, England to Melbourne, Australia.

The Australia I know is nothing like the country Brits see on Holiday commercials or soap operas like *Neighbours* and *Home & Away*. That's the beauty of living and working in a country over just visiting. Australia still feels like a young country, like you can come here and truly make something of your life and most do. It's so much more than sunshine and beaches, though if that's what floats your boat, you're in the right place for sure. I once read a quote that said after forty you care less and less about more and more every day. I *wish* I could. Instead, I feel more concerned about the World today than I ever did. I used to worry about getting my nails done for camera, about that red carpet dress. I used to stress about accepting the right social invitations and camera angles for press, my God it feels like a different lifetime, a totally different person. Now I live in a constant state of frustration with myself that I ever cared about any of those things. Yes they were fun, yes they saw me experience the things that everybody *thinks* they want, Fame and Money, and I am so grateful for that, because now I know that those things aren't important at all. Not having had the chance to form loving relationships when I was young meant that I set the bar very low when it came to how I was treated, by friends, by colleagues and by men. It saw me accept upsetting work environments and stick it out in marriages that clearly weren't going to work, but mostly it destroyed my faith in love and my ability to believe in myself. Creating the character of *Sarah Beaumont,* an alter-ego I could live through and hide behind for many years began a rebuilding of my inner confidence. She altered the entire World's perspective of me. I can enter any room or situation, at the hairdressers, at meetings, at the supermarket or at work, and I still see the same look in the eyes of those I meet, a look that betrays,

It's really her, it's really Sarah Beaumont, what will she do or say next?

and of being thrown down the stairs by a partner who was supposed to love me, I am convinced that I would not exist in the form I do now if I hadn't experienced those things. We are all survivors of *something*. I spent my life not expecting nice things to happen, and so barely knew how to recognize them when they did, instead the points on my graph that remain immovable stains on my soul are more often than not instances where I was made to feel less than, an emotion I could easily recognize and curl up inside its familiarity. In fact, as I am sure you can tell, I remained trauma bonded to my childhood abuse for the rest of my life, and many other negative experiences too because trauma teaches you to remember your lessons well. But the great thing about aging is that hindsight plucks the best and worst from every scenario and begs you to take a second look. Would I have done things differently? Sure, who wouldn't? Do I have regrets? Not many, but some. I wouldn't have left Neighbours and I wouldn't have moved my life to LA. Promise me you will value good luck when it comes along, for things can always get worse, and often do. I do know one thing for sure though, that truth is much stranger than fiction, especially when it comes to human behavior. Be careful how far down the rabbit hole you go, I find that sometimes, not knowing the truth about who or what those around you are, can protect your heart and soul. Perhaps the model from Wisconsin had something when she said she was happy to live in ignorance. I am grateful each morning to see the happy faces of my dogs, tails wagging as they remind me that not everything in this World is complicated.

(PHOTO: My beautiful female Boerboel "Tank Girl" and I in the Dandenong Ranges. She truly knows the meaning of the word Family and has been my constant companion for the past four years. I recently found her a partner of her own and

adopted Chewbacca, a happy-go-lucky male Boerboel who
lets her be the boss and spends his time following her around.)

(PHOTO: Tank Girl and Chewbacca. My haters are more
than welcome to come and spend five minutes with my dogs.)

I feel blessed to be loved by a man who took me by surprise and made the sun come up, and I am honored to be the Mother of my three incredible children Freya, Nova and Archie. These humans and creatures are far more valuable to me than any career achievement or accolade. I am also honored to have played *Miss Sarah Beaumont*. The femme fatale of Ramsay Street, Erinsborough, a fictional town that was tough to grow up in.

I am a fighter, and I fought through and survived it all. The dust has settled, and I'm still standing bitches, and the best part is living my life right here in Melbourne, Australia, the city that once upon a time made me a *SOAP STAR*.

The End.

Lightning Source UK Ltd.
Milton Keynes UK
UKHW021331290421
382828UK00005B/78